OECD DOCUMENTS

ENVIRONMENT AND TAXATION: THE CASES OF THE NETHERLANDS, SWEDEN AND THE UNITED STATES

PUBLISHER'S NOTE

The following texts have been left in their original form to permit faster distribution at lower cost.

ORGANISATION FOR ECONOMIC CO-OPERATION AND DEVELOPMENT

ORGANISATION FOR ECONOMIC CO-OPERATION AND DEVELOPMENT

Pursuant to Article 1 of the Convention signed in Paris on 14th December 1960, and which came into force on 30th September 1961, the Organisation for Economic Co-operation and Development (OECD) shall promote policies designed:

— to achieve the highest sustainable economic growth and employment and a rising standard of living in Member countries, while maintaining financial stability, and thus to contribute to the development of the world economy;

— to contribute to sound economic expansion in Member as well as non-member countries in the process of economic development; and

— to contribute to the expansion of world trade on a multilateral, non-discriminatory basis in accordance with international obligations.

The original Member countries of the OECD are Austria, Belgium, Canada, Denmark, France, Germany, Greece, Iceland, Ireland, Italy, Luxembourg, the Netherlands, Norway, Portugal, Spain, Sweden, Switzerland, Turkey, the United Kingdom and the United States. The following countries became Members subsequently through accession at the dates indicated hereafter: Japan (28th April 1964), Finland (28th January 1969), Australia (7th June 1971) and New Zealand (29th May 1973). The Commission of the European Communities takes part in the work of the OECD (Article 13 of the OECD Convention).

FOREWORD

Taxes are increasingly used for environmental purposes. Such "eco-taxes" take several forms such as taxes on polluting emissions and taxes on environmentally damaging products (e.g., pesticides, fertilizers, motor vehicles and fuels). In the context of the debate on global warming, the introduction of carbon taxes is high on the political agenda. On the other hand, existing tax structures may already be detrimental to the environment (for instance, inappropriate taxation of transport, energy and agriculture). Environmental and fiscal policies must therefore be properly integrated.

Governments are becoming increasingly aware of the potential gains in terms of both economic efficiency and environmental effectiveness that can be reaped with such an integration and appropriate reforms of existing tax systems. Indeed, a number of OECD countries have already implemented such fiscal reforms, while others are considering to do so.

In the context of a special OECD "Task Force on Taxation and Environment" consisting of representatives from both the Environment and Tax Departments of OECD Member countries, a work programme was carried out in 1991-92, in order to assess how, and to what extent, fiscal and environmental policies could be made, not only compatible, but also mutually reinforcing*. In this framework, the OECD commissioned case studies to carry out an in-depth analysis of this issue in four Member countries, namely France, the Netherlands, Sweden and the United States. The Three latter case studies are presented in this volume. The case study on France is published in French as *Environnement et fiscalité : le cas de la France*. The application of "eco-taxes" is reviewed in detail, as well as the key issues associated with these taxes such as earmarking of revenue, integration into the fiscal system, and the policy debate concerning these taxes.

These case studies are published under the responsibility of the Secretary-General.

---

* The findings and conclusion of this effort are published in OECD, *Taxation and Environment: Complementary Policies*, OECD, Paris 1993

ALSO AVAILABLE

Taxation and Environment: Complementary Policies

Eco-taxes in OECD Countries: A Survey

Environmental Policy: How to Apply Economic Instruments

Table of Contents*

_____

* Detailed tables of contents are presented with each case study.

ENVIRONMENT AND TAXATION:

THE CASE OF THE NETHERLANDS

(F.H. OOSTERHUIS and A.F. DE SAVORNIN LOHMAN
Institute for Environment Studies, Free University of Amsterdam)

Table of Contents

Chapter 1

OVERVIEW

1.1   Dutch environmental policy

From 1970 on Dutch environmental policy steadily evolved into an elaborate system of compartmental laws, separately dealing with air, water, soil, noise and waste removal. In 1989 environmental policy intensified with the National Environmental Policy Plan (NEPP), to be the first in a series of revolving integrated plans, involving a doubling of societal environmental expenditure up to 1994. With environmental problems increasingly transgressing compartments, a "thematic" approach has been initiated involving such themes as climate change, acidification, waste removal, and eutrophication. NEPP now is in its implementation phase, with progress differing among themes. In the recent 1992 budget statement the Ministry of the Environment stated eutrophication, waste removal and legislation enforcement to be the most pressing problems.

Also in the 1990-NEPP-plus "research and experiments" were announced on a series of product charges and deposit refund systems. In the recent 1992 budget statement considerable attention was devoted to the state of affairs in preparing the application of financial instruments.

1.2   Present role of economic instruments

Dutch environmental policy primarily consists of direct regulation and voluntary agreements with producers. The role of economic instruments has been rather limited until now, but this may change in the near future (cf. Ch. 3).

Environmental taxes and charges, extensively reviewed in 2.1., officially are only for financing environmental expenditure. Only the tax differentiations on non-leaded car gasoline and cars with catalytic converters serve an incentive purpose. According to research the water pollution charge[1], levied by the non governmental Water Boards as a user charge, has an incentive impact.

Subsidies are applied in energy policy, to promote conservation and renewables. In environmental policy subsidies fulfil a complementary role in making the medicine of direct regulation and voluntary agreements go down more easily.

Major subsidies are for energy conservation, CHP (combined heat and power), renewable energy sources, manure processing and storage, low emission vehicles, and low emission heating systems. There is a large range of minor subsidies, a.o. for clean technology R and D, excessive compliance cost and company environmental management systems.

There are deposit refunds on glass bottles (soft drinks, beer and milk) and on PET-bottles, instituted by industry itself. Environmental legislation as yet does not allow obligatory introduction of deposit refund systems, but this will be changed before long.

In the 1992 budget conditionally "return premium" systems are announced for aluminium cans, refrigerators, batteries and waste oil, in case voluntary agreements with industry do not attain policy objectives. So also in this case economic instruments are applied as a complement to the "core business" of direct regulation and voluntary agreements.

1.3.   Main features of the Dutch tax system

The Dutch tax system is characterized by two important starting-points: the "ability-to-pay" principle and the "direct benefit" principle. The first principle means that "the strongest shoulders should carry the heaviest burdens". The second principle implies that those who gain more than others from public goods should also pay more. Of course, these two principles are not always compatible and often a compromise between them must be found.

Total tax revenue in 1989 was nearly ƒ 125 billion (excluding social security contributions), of which nearly 95% went to the central government. This amounts to about 30% of NNI (if social security contributions are included, this figure is more than 50% of NNI). Direct and indirect taxes both account for about half of the tax proceeds. The main tax components are wage and income tax (ƒ 43 billion), value added tax (ƒ 35 billion) and corporate tax (ƒ 17 billion).

Environmental taxes amount to nearly ƒ 3 billion, which is less than 2.5% of total tax revenue.

12

Chapter 2

EXISTING TAXES AND THE ENVIRONMENT

This chapter gives a description of the most important fiscal instruments which are presently (October 1991) in use in the Netherlands and which (may) have an impact on the environment. Also, these instruments are briefly analysed to assess their (potential) economic and environmental effects. In section 2.1 the instruments with an explicit environmental objective will be reviewed. Section 2.2 contains taxes and tax provisions which may have (direct) environmental side-effects. Section 2.3 presents some concluding remarks.

2.1   Taxes designed for environmental purpose

2.1.1   *The environmental charge on fuels*

2.1.1.1   *Description*

Since April 1, 1988, the main financial resource for Dutch environmental policy is the charge on fuels. This charge replaces the previous charges on air pollution, noise, lubricant oils and chemical waste. Its primary goal is revenue raising.

The charge base and tariffs for 1991 are presented in table 2.1.

Furthermore, an incentive charge exists on leaded gasoline with an octane number of less than 97 (f 7.00 per hectolitre) and on unleaded gasoline with an octane number of less than 95 (f 3.00 per hectolitre).

Users of oil and coal who reduce their SO_2 emissions to less than $400g/m^3$ and achieve a desulphurization rate of at least 85% can get a partial charge refund of f 2.25 per 1000 kg oil or coal. This is a concession to the power plants which have invested in flue gas desulphurization in recent years.

The tariff difference between unleaded and leaded gasoline is meant as an incentive for the use of unleaded gasoline. Together with the difference in excise tax (see § 2.1.10), the total tax difference between leaded and unleaded gasoline is now f 0.14 per litre.

The tariff differences between gas oil for road traffic and for other purposes (mainly heating), and between natural gas for small and large users, have been introduced for distributional purposes. More generally, the tariff structure is based on distributional and political considerations,

13

rather than on the relative environmental impact of the various fuels. However, since 1990 a "CO_2 charge" is included in the above-mentioned charge rates. This part of the charge is based on the carbon content of the fuel. In the future, the relative rates will be based on carbon (50%) and energy content (50%).

The total expected revenue of the fuel charge for 1991 is f 926.3 million, of which f 150 million is the CO_2 charge.

Table 2.1 Charge base and 1991 tariffs for the Dutch fuel charge

Product	Unit	Tariff (f per unit)
Unleaded gasoline	hectolitre	2.38
Leaded gasoline	hectolitre	6.87
Medium-light oil	hectolitre	0.94
Gas oil (road traffic)	hectolitre	4.37
Heavy oil	1000 kg	23.18
Liquified petrol gas	1000 kg	10.68
Coal	1000 kg	22.54
(Coke) furnace gas, coal		
Gas, refinery gas	1000 GJ	163.21
Natural gas:		
- small users	1000 m^3	9.72
- large users	1000 m^3	9.49
(> 170,000 m^3)		
Petroleum coke (*)	1000 kg	25.35
Liquid fuels (*)	1000 kg	23.00
Gaseous fuels (*)	1000 GJ	163.21

(*) for use in petroleum and chemical industry

2.1.1.2   Evaluation

As said before, the main function of the fuel charge is to provide financial means for the Dutch environmental policy. Every year, the rates are determined, based on the estimated costs of certain legally fixed tasks of the Ministry of Environment. In this sense, the charge seems to function quite well.

The charges on "normal" leaded and unleaded gasoline of f7 and f3 per hl respectively have been introduced with an explicit incentive purpose. The Dutch government did not want to prohibit leaded gasoline by means of command and control, because she thought that EC regulations would not give space to the use of the instrument of direct regulation in this situation. Apparently, the former charge was as effective as a ban: "normal" leaded gasoline has vanished from the market. The latter charge has also been effective, because it stimulated the introduction of unleaded gasoline with an octane number over 95, the so-called "Eurosuper".

14

Presently, about 60% of the gasoline-fueled cars in the Netherlands uses lead-free gasoline. It is, however, impossible to say which part of this result can be attributed to the charge and tax differentiations between leaded and unleaded gasoline, which part to the tax reduction on cars with catalytic converters (q.v.), and which part to other factors.

The economic impacts of the charge are probably modest until now, because the rates have been designed purposely so as to prevent major shifts in the tax burden of specific sectors. The total revenue is less than 0.25% of GNP.

The enforcement costs of the fuel charge are relatively low, because the number of energy producers and importers is low, and the system can partly "hitch-hike" with the ordinary excise tax on oil products.

2.1.2   *Noise charge on civil aviation*

2.1.2.1   *Description*

Users of civil aeroplanes, landing at Dutch airports, are liable to a noise charge. In principle, the base of this charge is the share in the total noise production in a certain "noise zone" around the airport. The charge rate is calculated as follows:

-- for aeroplanes with a weight between 6000 and 20,000 kg:
   charge = F x (0.20 + 0.04W);
-- for aeroplanes with a weight above 20,000 kg:

   a) if noise levels within the noise zone are known:
      charge = F x n x 10 x $(L_r - 270)/45$;

   b) if noise levels are unknown:
      charge = F x k x $W^{2/3}$.

(Meaning of the symbols:
   F =   a factor which is determined once a year by the minister of transport, based on the revenues which are needed for measures against noise nuisance in that year. In 1991, the factor F is fixed at 32.
   W =   the weight of the aeroplane (in tonnes).
   n =   a correction factor which has to do with measuring positions and conditions; it can vary from 0.85 to 1.50.
   L_r =   the sum of the noise levels at the measuring positions.
   k =   a constant, dependent on the type of aeroplane. It can vary from 0.15 to 0.95).

The noise charge has no incentive function. It is intended as a source of financing for measures against noise nuisance in the "noise zones" around airports (sound-proofing facilities at houses; withdrawal of houses from residential purpose).

The charge revenue in 1989 amounted to *f* 17 million.

15

2.1.2.2 Evaluation

The noise charge does not seem to function very well. Many airline companies refuse to pay the charge. They argue that "noise zones" around civil airports have not yet officially been established. As the revenues of the charge may only be used for measures against noise nuisance in these zones, it is in their opinion impossible to impose the charge presently. The government is now trying to give the noise charge a stronger legal basis.

2.1.3   *Waste charge and refuse collection rate*

2.1.3.1 Description

Municipalities can impose a charge on private households to finance the costs of waste collection. They can choose between a waste charge and a refuse collection rate. The waste charge can be imposed on all households where waste can be produced regularly. The refuse collection rate can only be imposed if waste collection is actually being executed.

The waste charge can be differentiated according to the number of persons in a household and the frequency of waste collection, but not to the amount or the weight of the waste produced. The refuse collection rate, however, can take these latter quantities also into account. In practice, there are municipalities which levy their refuse collection rate by imposing a surcharge on (prescribed) refuse bags. The revenue of waste charge or refuse collection rate may not exceed the costs of waste collection and processing. The total revenue from both kinds of waste taxation amounted to ƒ 810 million in 1990.

2.1.3.2 Evaluation

Although both waste taxation systems are clearly meant as a financing instrument, the refuse collection rate may be used also as an incentive to reduce the amount of waste produced. Practical experience with surcharges on refuse bags shows that there are some important conditions which should be taken into account (VNG, 1990):

-- the financial incentive should be high enough to stimulate separation at the source;

-- there should be adequate facilities to enable separation at the source;

-- municipalities should anticipate on the possibility of "evasive behaviour" and diffuse waste.

Presently, there is a tendency towards the use of so-called "mini-containers" for waste collection. Experiments are being performed in which the refuse collection rate is linked to the weight of waste offered by a household, using bar codes to identify the mini-container.

Tariff differentiation brings about additional measuring and registration costs for the municipalities. It is expected that these costs can be compensated for by the lower amount of waste offered, if this decrease is at least 10 per cent.

2.1.4   The charge on water pollution

2.1.4.1   Description

The charge on water pollution can be imposed on everyone who emits waste substances, polluting or noxious substances directly or indirectly into surface water or into a collectively exploited water purification plant. The charge can be levied by public authorities or by Water Boards. The Water Boards (of which there are 30 in the Netherlands) are non-governmental bodies, governed by councils in which affected interests are represented. Their task is "quantitative" and "qualitative" water management of non-state waters. State waters include major rivers and sea basins.

The charge can be based on the quantity and/or the quality of the afore-mentioned substances. In practice, the charge is applied to discharges of oxygen consuming substances and (only for emissions to non-state waters) heavy metals. Both kinds of pollution are being expressed in so-called "pollution equivalents" (p.e.). One p.e. equals 136 grams of oxygen demand (for biodegradable matter), 1 kilogram of the heavy metals As, Cr, Cu, Pb, Ni, Ag or Zn, and 100 grams of Hg or Cd. The number of p.e.'s for households and small firms is fixed by the authorities. The emissions of larger firms are being assessed by means of a table of emission coefficients, or can be measured. Only in the latter case an incentive effect is to be expected.

The water pollution charge has primarily a financial purpose: it is intended to finance the costs of water purification. The charge rate for state waters is relatively low (f 35 or f 39.50 per p.e. in 1991), because the state does not exploit its own water treatment plants. Among Water Boards and other water management authorities, the rates vary considerably, depending on their purification costs. The average is presently f 60, the range is from f 35 to f 110 per p.e. per year. The total revenue of water pollution charges in 1989 was f 1,301 million.

For industrial sources, the charge is applied in addition to direct regulation.

2.1.4.2   Evaluation

Apart from being an important source of finance for water purification plants, the water pollution charge has also had a rather strong incentive effect (see Opschoor and Vos, 1989). In the 20 years of its existence, both the quality of waste water and the number of treatment plants have risen considerably (see table 2.2).

Table 2.2 Water pollution and purification in the Netherlands
(millions of pollution equivalents; heavy metals and
phosphates not included)

	1969	1990
Total emissions	45.4	23.6
Reduction in collective purification plants	5.5	17.4
Remaining pollution	40.0	6.2

Source: Jansen, 1991

Schuurman (1988) interviewed firms that had taken measures against water pollution in the period 1975-1980. For 43% of them, the water pollution charge had been the only reason for taking these measures. The resistance against the charge has declined, in spite of steadily increasing rates.

It must be added, however, that the problem of contaminated waste water has to a large extent been replaced by the problem of contaminated sludge (especially with heavy metals).

The perception costs of the charge are relatively low. All private households and small firms are being charged according to a fixed rate. Furthermore, many water quality managers can "hitch-hike" on the electricity bills for collecting the charge.

The economic consequences of the water pollution charge seem to be rather modest. Generally, the charge burden of enterprises is less than 2% of their production value. Some sectors have met serious financial problems caused by water purification investments, but these investments were usually required by direct regulation.

2.1.5 The charge for soil protection

2.1.5.1 Description

A charge for soil protection can be levied by the provinces from those who extract groundwater and have an interest in certain measures against soil pollution. The provinces can take these measures in areas where the soil deserves a special protection level.

The charge base is the amount of groundwater extracted. The charge rate must be based on the compensations which are being paid to those who see themselves confronted with disproportional high costs because of the above-mentioned measures. Until now, the charge has not yet been applied.

18

2.1.5.2. Evaluation

The charge for soil protection is a purely financial one. It constitutes an exception to the "polluter pays principle". It makes the "victim" pay for pollution prevention, because it is deemed inequitable if polluters in certain vulnerable areas would have to pay for measures which are not required from their colleagues outside these areas.

2.1.6   The groundwater charge

2.1.6.1   Description

Provinces can levy a groundwater charge from those who extract groundwater. The charge base is the amount of groundwater extracted. In 1989, the rates varied from f 0.0032 to f 0.0117 per m^3. A few provinces levy no groundwater charge at all. Total revenue of this charge for all provinces was f 4 million in 1990.

The revenues of the levy may be used for research, necessary for groundwater management, and for compensations (e.g., in case of withdrawal of a permit, or in cases where damage caused by a decrease in the groundwater level can not be attributed to an individual causer).

2.1.6.2   Evaluation

The groundwater charge is a purely financial instrument. It serves as a provincial tax and the revenues are earmarked for specific purposes. Recently, the government has suggested that the provinces might increase the charge rate and use the proceeds more often to compensate for the withdrawal of permits, especially in regions suffering from dehydration.

The charge rate is presently too low (less than 1% of the price of drinking water) to have any significant incentive or economic effect.

2.1.7   The charge on surplus manure

2.1.7.1   Description

A charge on surplus manure is levied from those on whose farm manure is being produced. The charge base is the amount of manure produced, measured in phosphate. The phosphate production is calculated from the number of animals on the farm, using fixed factors. In certain cases (e.g., if the farmer uses "low-mineral" feed) these factors can be lowered.

The total phosphate production as calculated is divided by the area of agricultural land of the farmer. This gives an average phosphate production per hectare. The charge rates are:

-- zero for the phosphate production below 125 kg per ha[2];

-- ƒ 0.25 per kg for the phosphate production between 125 and 200 kg per ha;

-- ƒ 0.50 per kg for the phosphate production above 200 kg per ha.

The rate can be reduced to ƒ 0.15 per ha if it concerns:

-- manure being sold to a user, based on a multi-year contract, provided this does not lead to a phosphate level above 125 kg per ha at the user;

-- dry poultry manure being sold;

-- manure being exported.

The proceeds of the charge were ƒ 38 million in 1989. The charge is intended to finance:

-- operational costs of the so-called "manure banks";

-- contributions by the "manure banks" in the costs of processing, destruction and transportation of manure;

-- infrastructural facilities for the efficient supply, transport, processing or destruction of surplus manure;

-- the enforcement of parts of the Manure Act.

2.1.7.2   Evaluation

The charge on surplus manure is part of a package of measures, intended to reduce the amount of minerals which are being brought into the environment by dumping manure. Since their introduction in 1987, these measures have at least succeeded in stopping the increase in mineral emissions to the environment. Although the charge on surplus manure has a principal financial objective, it may be a substantial financial burden to the individual farmer, especially in combination with the other measures. The average charge presently amounts to ƒ 500 per cattle farm, but in the intensive livestock breeding it can amount to several thousands of guilders per year. Probably, the tendential decrease in the number of farms can partly be attributed to the manure legislation, but it is impossible to single out the role of the surplus manure charge.

2.1.8   Accelerated depreciation

2.1.8.1   Description

Since 1 September 1991, accelerated depreciation may be applied to certain categories of means of production which can contribute significantly to the reduction of environmental problems (including the use of energy and raw materials). A 100% depreciation on these capital goods is possible as soon as commitments or production costs have been made. Only those means of production which are not yet in widespread use qualify for this fiscal facility. They are put on a positive list which will be revised regularly.

In 1992, *f* 80 million will be available for this instrument. This amount will increase to *f* 120 million in 1994. The minister can interfere if this budget threatens to be exceeded.

2.1.8.2   Evaluation

There have been some criticisms on the instrument of accelerated depreciation, mainly concerning its economic effects and its susceptibility to fraud. It has been argued, for instance, that primarily large and profitable companies will benefit, because of the tax differentiation in the corporate tax and, in so far as a company is submitted to the income tax, the progressive tax rate in the income tax. Also, the act is said to contain insufficient provisions against improper use. It is, for example, possible to lease the depreciated good to a non-tax payer who would not have benefited from the fiscal facility if he had bought the good himself.

The environmental consequences of the instrument are assessed more positively in general, because it is expected to stimulate investments leading to emission reductions which go beyond legal requirements. Furthermore, the penetration of new technologies on the market (generating experience and learning effects which may lead to improvements in the technology itself) can be eased by this financial incentive.

2.1.9   Differentiation in special tax on motor vehicles

2.1.9.1   Description

The special tax on motor vehicles (see § 2.2.2) is reduced for cars which fulfil certain emission requirements. Cars which meet the USA emission standards, as well as cars with a cylinder capacity above 2 litres which meet the (less stringent) European standards, get *f* 1700 discount. Cars with a cylinder capacity of 2 litres or less which meet the European standards get *f* 850 discount. The total amount of tax expenditure involved can be roughly estimated at *f* 500 million per year. This is financed by a raise of the special sales tax levied on all new cars.

2.1.9.2   Evaluation

The tax differentiation (in combination with the excise differentiation for leaded and unleaded gasoline) seems to be an effective instrument in facilitating the introduction of "clean" cars on the Dutch market. In 1990, 95% of the newly sold passenger cars in the Netherlands was equipped with a catalytic converter.

2.1.10   *Differentiation in excise on oil products*

2.1.10.1 Description

The excise tax on oil products (see § 2.2.1) is lower for unleaded than for leaded gasoline. The difference is ƒ 7.50 per hectolitre. On top of that, a temporary surcharge on the excise tax on leaded gasoline of ƒ 2.05 per hl is levied. For a complete picture of the excise rates on mineral oil, see table 3.

Assuming that presently about 15 million hl (half of the amount of gasoline sold in the Netherlands) is lead-free, the tax expenditure can be assessed at ƒ 150 million per year (when compared with a situation in which 100% of the gasoline would be leaded).

The excise difference has been introduced as an incentive measure. The instrument was chosen because a ban on leaded fuel was considered unfeasible by the Dutch government, because of EC regulations.

2.1.10.2 Evaluation

As said in the preceding section, the combination of tax differentiation for "clean" cars and leaded/unleaded fuel has been a successful instrument of environmental policy. Presently, about 60% of the gasoline-driven cars in the Netherlands uses lead-free gasoline.

2.1.11   *Tax relief for owners of nature areas*

2.1.11.1 Description

Several tax regulations in the Netherlands contain special provisions for the protection of certain nature areas. These areas (usually country estates with forests) can be designated by the ministers of Finance and Nature Conservation, according to the Nature Protection Act of 1928.

For the wealth tax, the value of these areas can be assessed according to their "designation value" instead of their market value. By "designation value" is meant the value which such an area would have if there were an obligation to conserve it for 25 years in the present state, without harvesting wood. Legal bodies who own such areas (so-called "country estate bodies") can be exempt from corporate taxation. For the income tax and the wealth tax, the activities, assets and liabilities of "country estate bodies" can be treated as activities, assets and liabilities of the joint shareholders.

This means that the shareholders will be taxed according to the "designation" value of their part of the body, not to the (higher) value of their share.

Country estates and nature areas, designated on the basis of the Nature Protection Act of 1928, are exempt from transfer tax. For the inheritance and gift tax, a lower rate than usual is applied. The amount of deduction is higher if the estate is open to the public.

Country estates and nature areas (also those which have not been designated on the basis of the Nature Protection Act) are exempt from the municipal immovable property tax. Houses on country estates are taxed according to their "designation value".

Data which are required to assess the amount of tax expenditure that can be attributed to the various regulations for country estates and nature areas are lacking.

2.1.11.2 Evaluation

The importance of the various fiscal instruments for nature areas and country estates is hard to assess. It is not very likely that these regulations will have a large impact on the way in which such areas are managed. In many cases, the owners will have the intention to maintain the character of the area anyway. Furthermore, the Physical Planning Act enables municipalities to designate areas for nature conservation, which can make the difference in value between the market value and the "designation value" of the area rather small.

2.2. Other taxes with (potential) environmental effects

In this section, some existing tax regulations are described which may have environmental side-effects. The subsections are arranged according to the kind of products or activities which may be affected, because one product or activity is often subject to several tax regulations.

2.2.1. Fuels

Apart from the environmental charge on fuels, there is an excise tax on mineral oil products. This excise yields a total revenue of nearly 5 billion guilders per year. It has no incentive purpose (except the differentiation between leaded and unleaded gasoline), but it may theoretically limit the demand for fuels by raising their market price. Table 2.3 gives the excise rates as from the 6th of July, 1991. Although the rates for gasoline are relatively high (about 50% of the sales price), the impact should not be overestimated, because of the low price elasticity of the demand for gasoline.

Table 2.3 Excise rates for oil products in the Netherlands

Product	Unit	Excise rate	COVA charge *
Light oil, leaded	hl	ƒ 104.65	ƒ 1.20
Light oil, unleaded	hl	ƒ 97.15	ƒ 1.20
Semi-heavy oil	hl	ƒ 10.26	ƒ 1.20
Gas oil (road traffic)	hl	ƒ 43.06	ƒ 1.20
Gas oil (other)	hl	ƒ 10.26	ƒ 1.20
Heavy oil	100 kg	ƒ 3.424	-

* The COVA charge is destined to finance emergency stockpiles.

Another effect of the excise structure may be a relatively high demand for gas oil (lower rate than gasoline) and LPG (no excise tax at all). The environmental impact of this demand structure is uncertain, as the emission characteristics of gasoline-driven cars are improving faster than those of cars using other motor fuels. Anyway, the motor vehicle tax for diesel and LPG cars is higher than for gasoline-driven cars, which may more or less compensate for the lower excises (depending on the distance driven per year).

2.2.2 Transport

Several tax provisions concern the costs of transport, especially those of commuting. Entrepreneurs may account for the costs of their own home-to-work transport as business costs. Employees can deduct these costs (partly) from their income for the income tax. The deductibility is higher for those who use public transport. If the employer pays a refund for commuting costs, the amount of compensation which is tax-free is also higher if the employee uses public transport, or if he has a carpooling-agreement. These fiscal benefits for public transport and carpooling have been introduced to reduce private car traffic, mainly because of traffic jams and air pollution.

Tax regulations may also influence the distance from home to work. For instance, it is sometimes argued that the transfer tax (6% of the value of a real estate transaction) hinders people to move closer to their work. On the other hand, it is also conceivable that people would move away from their work if buying a house were cheaper. The same ambiguity is present in the deductibility of moving costs (up to ƒ 12,000 per move) and in the municipal commuters tax. This latter tax can be imposed on those who have a house, but not their main residence in the municipality. This can be seen as an incentive to choose the municipality as their main residence (and hence to higher commuting distances), but it may also make people refrain from having a second house (thereby reducing mobility). However, as far as we know there has been no research on the impact of these taxes on residential choice.

24

As a general rule, the private use of business cars will be taxed as private income. If a business car is being used privately by an employee, at least 20% of the value of the car is being accounted for as income. If a private car is used for business purposes, only f 0.44 per km can be claimed as business costs. This is also the maximum amount that the employer can pay as a tax-free compensation.

Tax regulations which influence the relative prices of different means of transport are:

-- the motor vehicle tax: for passenger cars, this tax varies from a few hundred to several thousands of guilders per car per year, depending on the weight and the fuel used. Vehicles with an electromotor are exempted. There is also a temporary exemption for experiments with alternative fuels, like bio-ethanol, and for experiments with buses on natural gas. The total tax revenue amounted to f 3,605 million in 1989.

-- the special sales tax on passenger cars and motorcycles: for cars at least 18.5% of the sales price, for motorcycles at least 8% (with a reduction for "clean" cars; see § 2.1.9). Taxis are exempted. Total revenue was f 2,445 million in 1989.

-- the value added tax: cars and fuels are taxed according to the high rate of 18.5%; public transport according to the low rate of 6%.

Since 1.1.1991, municipalities can levy a parking tax (before that date it used to be a parking fee), which may be used as an instrument to limit the number of cars in city centres. Under the new tax instrument, municipalities have better enforcement possibilities.

2.2.3   Agriculture

Agricultural companies are exempt from corporate taxation if their profit is less than f 11,000 per year. This can be conceived of as a stimulus for small-scale agriculture, which is sometimes regarded as being environmentally benign. The relevance of this regulation is rather small, as most farms are family and not corporate enterprises.

Transactions within the framework of land consolidation plans or improvements in agricultural structure can be exempt from transfer tax. This may add to the promotion of large-scale agriculture.

Agricultural inputs like pesticides and fertilizers fall under the low VAT rate of 6%. This is for fiscal-technical reasons and has to do with the fact that agricultural outputs are also taxed according to the low rate. For firms which can deduct their paid VAT, this should have no influence on the use of these inputs[3]. For private users of pesticides and fertilizers, however, the low rate may be an incentive to use more of these inputs than if they would fall under the high rate.

2.2.4. Forestry

Profits from forestry are exempt from income and corporate taxation. This exemption is meant to stimulate the forest condition in the Netherlands. The environmental merit of this regulation is ambiguous. On the one hand, it may disencourage the conversion of forest areas into more environmentally harmful forms of land use. This aspect has only limited relevance, because most forests in the Netherlands are already protected by the Forest Act. On the other hand, it may work out as an incentive to harvest wood instead of managing the forest in a more nature-oriented way.

Forest areas are also exempt from the municipal immovable property tax. This may also be regarded as a disincentive to land use change (again, besides the Forest Act), although this does not hold true for a change into agricultural land (which is also exempt).

2.2.5 Hunting and fishing

For acquiring a hunting or fishing permit, a licence fee has to be paid. The present rates are ƒ 120 and ƒ 12.50 per year, respectively. There are about 30,000 hunters and 525,000 anglers in the Netherlands. The tax rates have no incentive purpose and are probably too low to have any effect on the number of people interfering with natural ecosystems by these activities.

2.2.6 Nature conservation

Gifts to institutions which pursue the general interest are tax-deductible, up to 10% of gross income. These gifts are also exempted from gift tax, if they do not exceed an amount of ƒ 6795. Higher amounts are taxed according to a special (low) rate of 11%. The same rate is applied in the inheritance tax for legacies to these institutions, exceeding an amount of ƒ 13,590. Environmental and nature protection groups can benefit from these regulations.

2.2.7 Other fiscal regulations

The municipal **dog tax** (revenue: ƒ 63 million per year) is probably the oldest tax with an explicit environmental incentive purpose. It has been introduced in the beginning of this century with the aim of limiting the number of dogs "to prevent the fouling of public places" (Maathuis, 1990). Presently, the incentive effect can be considered to be low.

Municipalities can also levy an **advertising tax** which may be used to combat visual pollution by public advertisement, although this instrument is nowhere being used as such, as far as the authors know.

Reservations and **liability entries** for environmental expenditures can be made on the balance sheet of a company, provided that there is a real chance that there will be an obligation (e.g., if the company is made liable by the state for soil pollution), or a strong expectation that the expenditures will be realized. The latter fiscal facility can be regarded as an incentive for voluntary soil cleaning.

Adminstrative **penalties**, including fines for the violation of environmental laws, are tax-deductible. This makes the factual financial effect of the penalty lower than the rate of the fine. However, administrative penalties or fines imposed by the tax administration because of not honouring the obligations with respect to environmental taxes or charges (or in general all taxes) are not tax-deductible. Penalties and fines imposed by the criminal judge are also not tax-deductible.

Import duties (uniform within the EC) have not been analyzed within the framework of this study. It will be hard to assess the environmental consequences of abandoning all tariff barriers. One might argue that the present situation, in which a lower rate is imposed on raw materials than on finished products, has a positive environmental impact, because production processes in the West are usually cleaner than in developing countries. On the other hand, a relatively low price for raw materials discourages recycling. Furthermore, destruction of tariff walls will lead to increases in world trade, with inevitably polluting transport streams.

2.3   *Concluding remarks*

Table 2.4 summarizes the results of § 2.1. For all taxes and tax provisions designed for environmental purposes it gives the amount of money involved in 1989 or 1990, as well as the main function: incentive (I) or revenue raising (R). If the incentive or revenue can be seen as a (significant) side-effect, a small letter is used. The performance of the tax (provision) as an environmental policy instrument is marked as positive (+), negative (-), or uncertain (0).

Table 2.5 is based on section 2.2 and shows how other taxes with (potential) environmental effects may work out on certain products and activities. The effect can be positive for the environment (+), negative (-), or uncertain (0). As there are practically no quantitative data to base this assessment on, the conclusions drawn here are rather speculative. Information on the amounts of money involved is largely absent.

Generally speaking, it is probable that presently only the fiscal regulations for the transport sector have any significant environmental effects, although the effects may be opposite. Any quantitative statements about the environmental merit-demerit balance of the present tax system will require substantial data collecting and research work. As yet, however, there is no evidence for the statement that the present Dutch tax system (apart from charging labour instead of pollution) is on balance detrimental to the environment.

Table 2.4 Taxes designed for environmental purpose

Tax	Amount (mln f)	Function	Performance
Environmental charge on fuels	926.3	R, I[*]	+
of which CO$_2$ charge	150.0	R	+
Noise charge on civil aviation	17.0	R	0
Waste charge and refuse collection rate	810.0	R	+
Charge on water pollution	1301.0	R, i	+
Charge for soil protection	0	R	**
Groundwater charge	4.0	R	0
Charge on surplus manure	38.0	R	+
Accelerated depreciation (1992)	8.0	I	0
Differentiation in special tax on motor vehicles	500.0	I	+
Differentiation in excise on oil products	150.0	I	+
Tax relief for owners of nature areas	?	I	0

---

[*] Incentive function only as far as the charge on low-octane gasoline is concerned.

[**] Not yet applied.

Table 2.5 Other taxes with environmental effects

Product/activity	Tax regulation	(Potential) Effect
Fuels	Excise	+/0
Transport	Fiscal facilities for commuting costs	-
	Idem: preferential treatment for public transport and carpooling	+
	Transfer tax	0
	Deductibility of moving costs	0
	Municipal commuters tax	0
	Tax on private use of business car	0
	Limit to deductibility of business trip costs	+
	Motor vehicle tax	+
	Special tax on passenger cars and motorcycles	+
	VAT: differentiation between private and public transport	+
	parking tax	+
Agriculture	Exemption from corporate taxation for small farms	0
	Exemption from transfer tax in case of land consolidation	-
	Low VAT rate for pesticides and fertilizers	-
Forestry	Exemption from income and corporate tax	0
	Exemption from municipal immovable property tax	0
Hunting and fishing	Hunting and fishing licence fees	0
Nature conservation	Deductibility and tax reduction of gifts and legacies to environmental and nature protection organizations	+
Other	Dog tax	+
	Advertising tax	+
	Allowance of reservations and liability entries for environmental expenditures	+
	Deductibility of environmental fines	-
	Import duties	0

Chapter 3

THE ENVIRONMENTAL POLICY DEBATE ON TAX INSTRUMENTS

Recently, since the parliamentary debate about the 1992 budget, the Dutch political debate about taxation and environmental policy has intensified.

3.1   The state of affairs in april 1992

Concerning tax-based instruments the core elements coming out of the parliamentary debate on the 1992 environmental budget are:

1. A draft law is in preparation with the aim to introduce taxes on an environmental basis. Possible taxable objects are (ground)water, household waste, pesticides and agricultural nutrients. Any revenues will go to the general budget.

    The General Fuel Charge[4] will change from an earmarked charge to a general fuel tax, to be executed by the Ministry of Finance and revenues flowing into the general budget.

    In 1991 the GFC had a Dfl. 900 mln. revenue. The intention is to raise the revenues from environmental taxation (GFC and other) up to Dlf. 1500 mln. in 1992 and Dfl. 2200 mln. in 1993 (appr. 0.4% of GDP).

    Also the budget of the Environment Ministry is expanded up to 1993 with Dfl. 600 mln.

2. Ongoing preparations for the application of financial instruments (taxes and deposit refunds). The 1992 budget set out a policy framework for assessing financial instruments in environmental policy (3.1.2).

3. A rise of gasoline and vehicle taxes, revenues to be allocated to the general budget (3.1.3).

In the budget statement the present insuffiency of law enforcement is recognized as a major theme. The issue has been raised before, and as yet has primarily resulted in additional spending on enforcement agencies and the continued use of voluntary agreements with producers. No link has been made yet with positive enforcement characteristics of economic instruments.

3.1.1　Energy taxation

The budget statement pinpoints January 1st 1993 as the ultimate date for deciding on an incentive charge on energy products. In february 1992 the "Wolfson-committee", consisting of civil servants and independent experts reported on the pro's and cons of energy taxation. Three options have been scrutinized:

1. A 50% and a 100% OECD-wide charge on all use of primary energy on the basis of 50% CO_2-emission and 50% energy content;

2. A 50% and a 100% charge on all primary energy use in the Netherlands on the basis of 50% CO_2-emission and 50% energy content;

3. A 50% and a 100% charge on primary energy (excluding feedstocks) in the Netherlands by small users (households and small industry) based on the market price of the energy product. Motor fuels are excluded because of expected border effects.

Revenue neutrality is presupposed.

The commission's report describes the "corners of the playing field". The three options are not intended to be implemented as such, but the results of the these options can play a role in the decision-making as to whether or not an energy tax in any form should be introduced in the Netherlands.

3.1.2　Specific incentive charges and the policy framework

In May 1990 the NEPP-plus announced "research and experiments" on a series of specific incentive charges, mostly on products. As yet introduction has not taken place. The 1992-budget only announced a financing charge on pesticides (for R&D).

Charges on short cycle PVC, laminated packaging, metal degreasers and car wrecks are rejected as non-feasible. Research is continuing on the feasibility of charges on light bulbs, paint based on organic solvents, agricultural emissions of minerals, pesticides and surface minerals.

Charges on disposable products, waste from the service sector, drinking water and blasting grit will be introduced if present policies, mainly based on voluntary agreements with producers, appear to be insufficiently effective.

The 1992 budget sets out an elaborate "policy framework" for assessment and stepwise preparation of economic instruments. It is a specific feature of taxation as a policy instrument, that it forces the Environment Ministry into dealings with Finance and Economic Ministries. The policy framework states as a primary condition that instruments should be environmentally effective and administratively feasible.

Second, effects on purchasing power, competitiveness and employment have to be taken into account, charges should fit in with the general budgettary framework (which now puts a ceiling to the aggregate collective charge level) and be fiscally acceptable.

The extensiveness of the policy framework - usually in environmental policy such elaborate criteria are not applied - may be an indicator of bureaucratic reluctance on the issue of environmental taxation.

3.1.3   Transport and environment

In the 1992 budget gasoline and vehicle taxes are raised. Simultaneously tariffs for public transport are raised, to finance increased infrastructure investment[5] and cut spiralling public transport subsidies in a general effort to cut subsidies.

Variabilisation of motoring costs, differentiation of vehicle taxes on environmental grounds, tax differentiations favouring clean trucks and low-sulphur diesel oil are being studied. An environmental impact assessment of the fiscal regime for deducting commuting expenses is envisaged.

Implementation plans for road pricing are still being prepared. In the recent past a plan for computerized road pricing has been withdrawn, as well as a preliminary proposal for peak hour pricing. According to in 't Veld (1991) the withdrawn road pricing proposal fell victim to strongly held preferences for the status quo (roads as free goods) as well insufficienct mobilisation of supporters and the "the paradox of effectiveness": effective proposals are rejected just because they are really painful. A coalition of professional and private road users, garage owners, local authorities (fearing overloading of secondary roadways) and politicians arguing against distributional impacts on specific low income groups beat the proposal, which was only weakly supported by environmentalists and the public transport sector.

3.2   Non governmental actors

In recent statements the influential Social Economic Council, composed of employers, trade unions and independent experts, suscribed to the need for sustainable economic development and pleaded for the application of financial incentives in environmental policy. Revenues of incentive charges should be returned to taxpayers, and in cases of excessive damage to competitiveness temporal compensation is to be considered. The Netherlands should actively promote financial incentives internationally. Fiscal harmonisation in the EC should take into account environmental considerations, implying "high" taxes on energy products.

In separate statements the largest employers' associations VNO and NCW took a more reserved attitude, explictly preferring direct regulation and subjecting incentive charges to a set of strict conditions.
Environmental associations, suspicious of economic incentives in the past, now are increasingly coming out in favour of financial incentives.

On the issue of an energy *incentive charge* positions of critical actors are summarily reviewed below, as an example to illustrate the complexities of the socio-political field of forces in a specific case of environmental taxation.

Industry prefers subsidies and voluntary agreements for energy conservation. If a charge is introduced, European harmonisation is a precondition and revenues should be returned to taxpayers. Energy intensive branches subject to international competition should be compensated.

Political parties are lukewarm, having a hard time in explaining the concept of incentive taxation to voters and disagreeing about modalities of compensation.

Energy distribution companies[6] object to incentive charges, regarding them ineffective, inequitable and unnecessary government interference in energy matters. Presently energy distribution companies are carrying out their own "Environmental Action Plan", financed by a 1-2% surcharge on tariffs.

Environmental groups have pleaded for a tax doubling energy prices. Consumer associations object to income effects, arguing that many users can hardly reduce their energy use due to landlord tenant problems, limited financing means and individual circumstances (age, handicaps).

Chapter 4

ASSESSMENT

4.1   Fiscal compatibility of environmental taxation[7]

4.1.1   Neutrality: principle and practice

Fiscal neutrality, the cornerstone of various recent tax-reforms in OECD-countries, is a valuable concept if used to safeguard the integrity of tax systems from special interest groups in society and ephemeral political objectives. From a fiscal point of view broad legitimacy and revenue raising are primary. The neutrality principle throws up a dam against permanent pressures for turning the tax system into a pork barrel for interest groups and politicians.

On the other hand the neutrality principle is carried too far, if it is used as an unqualified defense of the status-quo. There is nothing "natural" about prevailing market prices, as they do not take into account external effects, may yield distributional outcomes unanimously regarded unacceptable[8] and cannot provide collectively desired public goods.

Is environmental taxation at variance with the neutrality principle?

It does not favor the material interests of a special interest group, but reflects environmental values benefiting the whole of society. Environmental protection is not an ephemeral objective originating from the political scene, but is now widely recognized as fundamental for the sustainability of industrial economies.

Environmental taxation reflects the principle of internalising external costs, which is not a contingent political objective, but a principle of *equity* within civil society[9].

Therefore environmental taxation is not at cross-purposes with fiscal neutrality *in principle*.

As *operational* criteria for accepting non-fiscal objectives, and designing taxes with non-fiscal objectives, have been proposed[10]:

1. Non-feasibility of alternative instruments to attain the non-fiscal objective.
    According to this criterion environmental taxes are acceptable if alternative policy instruments are either ineffective, administratively unwieldy or too burdensome on society.

2. Acceptable administrative cost.
   Administrative cost, for taxing agencies as well as those paying the tax, should not be excessive. It is a matter for debate whether the acceptability standard should be derived from the practice of taxation or environmental policy. The view taken here is that the relevant comparison is with administrative cost of environmental policy, as non-implementation of the tax would imply the need for an alternative instrument of environmental policy, not an alternative tax.

3. Transparency and simplicity.
   Environmental taxes should be designed transparently and unambiguously, just as any tax. Complexity of tax bases hampers implementation; anyhow striving for perfection in environmental tax bases is of dubious value in view of the inherent complexity of ecosystems.

4. Concordance with supranational legislation.
   This is especially relevant for EC-member states. According to the European Act environmental policies of member states should not erect direct barriers to trade, discriminate against imports or materially favour domestic industry.

Traditionally taxation for non-revenue raising purposes is a bone of contention between fiscalists and welfare economists.

Fiscalists are trained as practitioners, to safeguard the essential revenue raising function and therefore focus on legitimacy and implementability. In a fiscalist view neutrality is equated with equality before the law, non-favoritism and avoidance of government power abuse. The intention of the tax-legislator is of imperative significance, as this is a determining factor for legitimacy.

Economists, theoretically inclined and taking legitimacy for granted, have little interest in intentions, but focus on effects. In the economic view there is no such thing as neutral taxation, as any tax induces economic agents to economize on the tax base. So taxes should be levied on undesirable items, such as polluting emissions or products, not on desirable ones such as labour income.

It would be of practical use if parties in the debate try and get a clear view of their respective biases as well as the merits of the other position. Both perspectives are internally valid, and should be put together in practical policy making.

4.1.2   Revenue stability

Environmental taxation induces producers and consumers to economize on products or emissions constituting the tax basse. Does this necessarily imply instability of revenue?

The answer to this question hinges on the attainable quality of short and long run revenue elasticity estimates. For small and specific items reliable elasticity estimates may be hard to obtain, especially for the long run in view of the uncertain pace of technical developments. For larger items, such as energy products and energy-related emissions, elasticity estimates have proved to be all but impossible.

Nevertheless, it is to be expected that revenues of environmental taxes are less stable than tax revenues related to macro-economic aggregates, such as income and value added taxes. If technical developments result in progressively declining revenues, tax rates can be raised, which is acceptable if the initial rate is set below the optimal level. Alternatively new environmental taxes can be levied, if these are warranted by objectives of environmental policy and have been properly prepared.

4.2   Taxes as environmental policy

Presently in OECD-countries environmental policy is implemented primarily by direct regulation. There has been a theoretical and practical debate on the relative merits of *charges versus standards*, that cannot be reviewed here in its extensiveness. Some of the major results are:

1. There is no general verdict on static effectiveness and efficiency.
    Actual effectiveness and efficiency depend on details of instrument design, implementation, monitoring and enforcement and time/space dimensions of environmental problems. Taxes can be designed and implemented just as imperfectly as direct regulation.
    Theoretically taxing emissions is preferable, but in view of complexities of monitoring and enforcement taxing products (eventually giving rebates for abatement) may be the only feasible way. Time/space dimensions of environmental problems may require backstop physical regulation.

2. Transition costs are important.
    Policy mixes, either combining direct regulation and taxation, or steadily phasing in tax based policies, may be required to cope with transition costs.

3. Standards offer lower environmental risk, taxes lower economic risk.
    Standards clearly denote environmental objectives, but may confer excessive costs on industry as policy makers' knowledge of polluters' compliance costs is imperfect. Taxes effectively put on a ceiling on compliance cost, but leave the attainment of the environmental objective to decisions of polluters.
    So the choice is one of preferred risk, dependent on the relative steepness of damage and abatement cost functions as perceived by the policymaker. If the damage function is relatively steep, for instance in case of toxicity, standards are preferable. If damages are uncertain, and cost functions are steep, for instance in climate change, taxes are the better instrument.

4. Incentives for technical change are crucial.

Many of the present environmental problems cannot be solved with the present state of technology. Therefore the superior incentive of taxation for technical change is of crucial importance. In theory so-called technology forcing standards can serve the same purpose, but in practice environmental authorities have insufficient knowledge of technical feasibilities and are under political pressure to apply technology forcing standards leniently once enforcement is due.

5. Environmental taxes create welfare gains as they are non-distortive, while existing taxes are.

Revenues of environmental taxes can be used to diminish existing distortive taxes, resulting in non-environmental welfare gains.

Textbook optimality has become qualified in the debate, but a general case for environmental taxation can still be made as a *no-regret policy in environmental policy fields beset by uncertainties*. If adequate specification and severity of an environmental problem is uncertain, taxation minimizes economic risks (3), gives incentives for technical change (4) and creates non-environmental welfare gains (5).

4.3 Setting the tax rate

The textbook prescription of setting tax rates to equalize marginal social damages and abatement costs, is difficult to apply in practice.
Practical alternatives are:

1. Relating the tax rate to a specific environmental target.

This procedure requires an estimation of compliance cost. If this is done incorrectly, either under- or overshooting will occur. Setting the rate by trial and error may be a costly affair in view of irreversibilities.

So taxation involves uncertainty about the attainment of the environmental target. Complementarily, if direct regulation is applied incomplete knowledge of compliance cost involves economic risks (4.2).

2. Bridging the price gap to a desired substitute

Combining a tax with a subsidy on the environmentally superior substitute can be done in a revenue neutral manner. In many OECD-countries product tax differentiation is applied for leaded and non-leaded gasoline; also in various countries annual duties or sales taxes are differentiated according to environmental characteristics of vehicles. However, if market prices are volatile the rate of differentiation has to be continually adapted.

Also with emission taxation a revenue neutral tax-subsidy regime is conceivable, rebating tax revenues to polluters by subsidizing abatement equipment. However practically devising adequate subsidy regimes is difficult, either requiring the establishment of a pollution benchmark or requiring separate identification of the environmental component in company investments.

4.4   Monitoring and enforcement

As practical difficulties of monitoring and enforcement are one of the major drawbacks of existing direct regulation policies, it is a crucial question whether taxes on emissions or products fare any better on this score.

Concerning *emission taxation* the record is mixed. Enforcement of permits ultimately relies on the non-credible sanction of firm closure. Also firms are induced to stall, as sanctions (if applied at all) take effect considerable time after the offence allowing firms to reap non-compliance benefits before the sanction is due, and tend to be not proportional to the environmental damage inflicted.

Direct regulation generally involves such ambiguous principles as Best Practical Means or Best Technical Means, involving environmental authorities in conflicts about the economic and technical feasibility of specific technologies of which polluting firms always have superior knowledge.

Emission taxation bypasses this type of conflict, offering firms the option of paying in stead of abating. Tax bills usually keep piling up in case of non-compliance, so the inducement to stall is not present. But the demands on monitoring are high as the exact amount of the emission has to be established for the tax liability.

The crucial practical question is to what implementational relationship between regulatory authorities and polluters permit or taxation systems lead. It has been argued that direct regulation by permit giving is an all-or-nothing type of policy - firms have no choice but to comply with the standard - establishing a polarized relationship between regulators and regulatees. On the other hand with taxation out of pocket costs for firms are higher, creating incentives for firms to disguise emissions.

Either way authorities may have substantial discretion in this. Experience with implementation of the Dutch water pollution charge indicates that a non-legalistic, consultative attitude of enforcing officers can do a lot of good[11].

Product taxes can be administered by regular tax authorities, making them an attractive option from the point of view of monitoring and enforcement.

Product taxes can be combined with rebates for abatement, thus approaching the theoretical ideal of emission taxation[12].

4.5   Distributional impacts

Environmental taxation reflects the so-called extended PPP-principle, as polluters are made to pay for the full use of the environmental resource. The standard OECD-PPP principle is less stringent, polluters paying for pollution abatement as prescribed by environmental authorities while leaving remaining emissions free of charge. Therefore distributional impacts of environmental taxation are more substantial in principle and the question of compensation is raised.

Whether compensation should be offered to polluters can be regarded as a normative question, but also as one of political and economic expediency.

Normatively compensation has been defended on the ground that environmental taxation constitutes a legislated shift of property rights. Such a constitutional change would justify compensation for harmed agents, especially if the legislation process involves majoritarian decisionmaking.

Political expediency can be invoked to justify permanent compensation in order to cope with polluters resistance, while offering society the favourable allocational effects induced by the tax. This type of compensation can serve a useful function in avoiding the by no means uncommon, but allocationally unjustified compromise of mitigating environmental targets. Anyhow, practice demonstrates that politically succesful taxation schemes do involve some type of compensation[13].

Economic expediency may justify temporal compensation in order to minimize transition costs, which may be substantial because of capital losses and required labour force adjustments (retraining and relocation).

Two types of distributional impacts can be distinguished. On the one hand there are impacts on personal income distribution, which are of significance only in the case of taxes on major consumption items, such as energy products. On the other hand there are distributional impacts on producers, as a group and individually, which are significant with any tax scheme.

The impact of product taxation on the distribution of personal income depends on the relative share of the product charged in consumption baskets of income groups.

Taking the case of energy products, available studies show environmental taxation to be regressive. Tax revenues can be used for compensation, but due to substantial intra-income-group differences in energy use compensation through the tax system can only be imperfect.

Alternative compensational devices would be:

*   exempting a specific minimum usage from taxation, keeping the marginal incentive intact;
*   non-monetary compensation, for instance by energy efficiency investments in public housing.

Compensation to producers can be provided through the tax system on a generic basis, for instance by lowering profit taxes or social security contributions. Whether and how the tax system can be used to provide compensation to specific branches or producers without breaching equal treatment principles, is dubious. The alternative is to allocate revenues to a policy of industrial restructuring, such as ultimately required by environmental targets.

4.6   International aspects

Emission taxation is cost-augmenting for polluters, just as direct regulation. With emission taxes out of pocket costs for industry are higher, but aggregate abatement expenditure is lower. If the tax revenue is rebated to industry collectively, aggregate international competitiveness is better than with the standards policy.

Product taxes on non-tradable consumer products do not affect national competitiveness, just as taxes on consumer tradables if an equal tax is levied on imported products.

A product tax on major industrial inputs, such as energy, does affect trading patterns. Therefore coordinating such taxes within trading blocs, such as the EC, is warranted to avoid trade deflection. However the smaller the economic significance of the input and the higher transport costs, the smaller the probability of actual deflection. So there is no need for full-fledged harmonisation in each and every case.

Within trade blocs subgroups of member-countries may choose to go ahead, on the basis of the subsidiarity principle if they strongly value the environmental damage involved, or to prepare their domestic industries for the strict environmental regulation they regard unavoidable in the long run.

EC-legislation does not in principle preclude member states from applying national levies. If EC-regulation exists, member states can apply stricter policies such as exclusively national levies, on the basis of art. 100A or 130T of the European Act. If there is no EC-regulation the sole criterion for acceptability is whether, directly or indirectly, barriers to trade are involved, to be judged on a case-by-case basis.

4.7   Macro-economic performance

The macro-economic impact of environmental taxes depends on the impact of the tax itself and spending of the revenue. Available models[14] calculating the impact of a CO_2-tax with full revenue recycling indicate just minor macro-impacts. As distortive taxes can be reduced and environmental efforts may entail economic benefits (reducing resource costs) such a result is not implausible. Of course on branch level substantial reallocations do occur.

Inflatory effects or impairment of profits can occur if new environmental taxes are shifted in wage bargaining. The extent of shifting is dependent on institutional arrangements in wage bargaining, for instance the price index used[15]. Governments may choose to intervene in wage bargaining to stop environmental cost-push inflation from developing, or unilateral shifting of environmental costs on profits.

It is important to keep in mind that for getting a full view of their merits, macro-economic impacts of environmental taxes should be evaluated either compared to a benchmark environmental policy, or including estimates of environmental benefits.

4.8   Earmarking

Earmarked charges are economically well-founded if the "benefit principle" applies, that is if those paying the charge exclusively benefit from the spending of the revenues, for instance in the case of road tolls.

To apply the benefit principle in environmental policy also the "causation principle" has to be invoked, holding those emitting damaging substances accountable. In this manner the levying of *user charges* for collective treatment, such as in water purification and waste oil handling, can be justified.

The environmental merits of collective treatment financed by user charges depend on the possibilities to dispose of collective treatment effluents without environmental damage.

User charges can be levied parafiscally, by non-governmental institutions in charge of managing an environmental resource. Such institutions, with strong legal and technical expertise, due representation of affected interests and at armslength of (the vagaries of) the political process do function already in water and waste management[16].

Earmarking is also involved in the case of tax-subsidy schemes, in which a tax is set below the optimum allocational level and revenues are earmarked for subsidies on abatement. Compared to environmental taxation the aggregate tax burden is higher, the benefits of reducing distortive taxation are foregone and incentives for technical advancements are lower. These drawbacks must be balanced against the advantages of less incisive distributional and economic impacts.

Earmarking revenue for subsidies, and collective treatment as well, has been criticized as implying a non-preventative type of environmental policy. Subsidies, apart from conflicting with the PPP-principle, in practice are biased towards end-of-pipe treatment and are difficult to design and implement adequately. Collective treatment is end-of-pipe by its very nature.

A more principled position towards earmarking is conceivable, rejecting earmarking altogether as introducing rigidities into the budgettary process. Does earmarking restrict the policymaker unduly in balancing the relative benefits of different types of expenditure?

The answer to this question depends on the view taken of the policymaker. Implicit in the anti-earmarking position are two questionable assumptions:

1. *The policymaker is a "benevolent dictator", maximizing social welfare according to a known social welfare function.*

   The theoretical validity of the concept of a social welfare function is a disputed issue in welfare economics. Anyhow, elections are anything but a perfect mechanism to finds its shape and parameters.

   If either of these points is taken, the benevolent dictator is in trouble: legitimacy is at stake. Alternative mechanisms are required to establish it and earmarking revenues is one such mechanism, as it constitutes the nearest thing to a "direct buy" by the electorate, establishing a quid pro quo between taxes and expenditure[17].

2. *The political process can and does comprehensively and rationally balance the benefits of expenditure alternatives.*

   In reality however budgettary decisionmaking is incrementalist, a.o. because of information imperfections. So in actual fact rationality in budgettary decisionmaking is partial.

   Even more critically, budgettary decisionmaking is influenced by special interest groups differently bestowed with lobbying resources, information and capabilities for free rider containment. Environmentalist pressure groups are at a disadvantage in this process because of their low capability for free rider containment. Also environmental groups tend to be excluded from government-industry bargaining circuits and are not represented on influential corporatist bodies. Therefore the extent to which environmental preferences of the electorate can effectively be expressed in the political and budgettary process is limited.

   An earmarked environmental tax would be a device to bind the hands of the policymaker in the name of the electorate, bypassing the really existing imperfections of the budgettary process.

4.9   Obstacles to environmental taxation

According to Opschoor and Vos (1989) environmental taxation effects is rarely applied in OECD-countries for attaining incentive effects; revenue raising is the primary motive. Why is it that a policy instrument, potentially providing environmental protection at minimum cost, is so unpopular?

For policy instruments to be feasible as well as practically effective the institutional context is of paramount importance[18]. It appears that incentives of critical actors in the environmental policy process are unfavorably disposed towards environmental taxation. *Industry* and *environmental bureaucrats* are satisfied with prevailing direct regulation policies. Also in the *political arena* environmental taxation is at a disadvantage, and *constitutional and legal obstacles* may pre-empt the adoption of taxation schemes.

Industry objects to the extended Polluter Pays Principle implicit in environmental taxation. Also industry is generally afraid that environmental objectives will serve as a convenient political legitimation for imposing additional tax burdens. Compared to taxation the process of implementing and enforcing direct regulation offers more scope for administrative discretion, allowing industry the opportunity to bargain for favourable treatment.

Administrative discretion is attractive also for environmental bureaucrats, who prefer "hard and fast" direct regulation policies actually allowing them wider discretion.
For environmental bureaucrats incentives are towards forcing maximum pollution abatement at *minimum visible* economic impact. According to interviews with environmental bureaucrats abstract "economic efficiency" is not prominent in their objective function[19]. In environmental bureaucracies legal and technical professionals predominate, while economists tend to reside in staff-departments isolated from regular decisionmaking[20].

An additional complication is that taxation compels environmental bureaucrats to share competence with fiscal branches of government. Fiscal bureaucrats are reluctant in admitting non-fiscal objectives in tax systems (4.1.1). On the other hand fiscal bureaucrats may welcome the revenue, however fearing revenue instability (4.1.2).

In the political arena environmental taxes have the unattractive feature of "invisible" economic benefits versus visible political costs. Benefits are abstract savings in compliance cost and opportunity costs of existing distortive taxes, however political costs involve the obvious distributional impacts of the tax. Tax revenues can be used for compensation, but losers are inevitable and these may outweigh winners in the political process.

In the political process there may be procedural obstacles, taxation proposals being treated in fiscal subcommittees of parliament, while proposals for direct regulation are treated by more favorably disposed environmental subcommittees. Requirements of accountability may preclude setting tax rates on the basis of complex and contestable calculations of marginal costs or elasticity[21].

Constitutionally any spatial differentiation of emission tax rates, required to avoid hot spots, may be precluded by tax legislation. Also environmental statutes may preclude taxation schemes, for instance by prescribing technologically based regulation.

4.10   Overcoming obstacles

The preceding section stressed the importance of political and institutional obstacles[22].

The political feasibility of environmental taxation can be enhanced by creating pressure for change, involving change agents, addressing the issue of compensation, designing (imperfect but) practical proposals and removal of constitutional and procedural obstacles (4.9).

As political decisionmaking is incremental, the political agenda is limited and critical actors are satisfied with direct regulation specific and well-timed pressure for change is required. Pressure can be initiated from the fiscal and the environmental side.

Fiscally environmental taxes offer better chances in times of budgettary problems[23], or if a necessity arises to reduce existing taxes in line with international agreements. Environmental taxation can be turned into the political issue of fiscal reform by promoting a growing awareness of the distortions created by existing taxes.

Economic efficiency is not a self evident issue in the political process. So the fundamental question is how to get it on the political agenda. Ambitious environmental targets and a political commitment to stick to these, can effectively put the issue of economic efficiency on the agenda. Observers agree that due to the ambitious environmental targets of the Clean Air Act, EPA and US industry were prompted to go for the cost saving mechanism of tradable permits.

Also the ineffectiveness of existing command and control legislation, requiring spiralling expenditure on monitoring and enforcement, can be turned into a case for environmental taxation.

Without flesh-and-blood change agents in the political or bureaucratic system, taking a vested interest in the subject, taxation proposals may not get far. In Sweden a parliamentary committee for proposing specific environmental charges was created in the late eighties, offering high political visibility to its members. In Finland a strong bureaucratic committee fulfils a comparable function. In the US pressure from politicians has enhanced the position of economic staff departments within EPA[24].

There is no way around the issue of compensation. As incentive taxation involves the extended Polluter Pays Principle and thus has substantial distributional impacts, disregarding these is a recipe for failure. Making polluters pay for the full value of the environmental resource according to the extended PPP is best regarded as un ultimate objective, not as the first step.

Without undoing the intended environmental incentive, a variety of compensation schemes is feasible. Compensation schemes adressing fundamental equity concerns, avoiding clearly identifiable losers can widen political support for environmental taxation, as well as "policy packages" providing linked benefits in other policy fields.

Practical proposals are called for, taking into account the ecological complexities of the policy field and accomodating practical difficulties of implementation, monitoring and enforcement. Due to the scientific and institutional complexities involved, in environmental policy "second best" is an ambitious objective.

Existing policy frameworks cannot simply be dismissed, as proper administration requires the heeding of legitimate expectations raised before, costs of transition may be substantial and implementational practice cannot be changed overnight.

Notes

1.   Bressers (1983), Schuurman (1988).

2.   125 kg phosphate per ha is the provisional standard in the present eutrophication policy. As there is a zero rate below 125 kg/ha, the charge is called a "surplus charge".

3.   To complicate things further, there is a special regulation which enables agriculture to be exempt from VAT payment. This means that these farmers also cannot deduct VAT paid on inputs, which could make a higher VAT rate effectively raise their input prices. On the other hand, if this would mean that the total VAT they paid would be higher than the VAT received, they would not apply for VAT exemption, because in that case they could have part of their VAT paid being refunded.

4.   The General Fuel Charge is a charge on energy products for financing environmental expenditure (see section 2.1.1).

5.   In the "Second Traffic and Transport Structure Scheme" public transport infrastructure investment was prioritized to road extensions.

6.   In the Netherlands these are independent from production companies.

7.   In this chapter "environmental taxation" refers to taxation with incentive purposes. Earmarked charges are treated separately in 4.8.

8.   The non-fiscal objective of income redistribution is accepted in many OECD-countries.

9.   Interestingly, environmental liability is increasingly figuring in *civil* law suits.

10.   Hofstra (1985), VROM (1991).

11.   Water board monitoring officers have ample technical expertise and actively seekt to advice firms on abatement technologies. Also in one case a tax liability was postponed, hypothecating it for financing investment in abatement equipment (Huppes and Kagan (1989)).

12.   An example of this approach is the rebate on the Dutch general energy charge if SO_2 reducing measures are taken (see section 2.1.1).

13.   Tietenberg (1991), Rolph (1983) and Zeckhauser (1984).

14.   Mors (1991) provides a useful overview.

15.   In the Netherlands environmental user charges for water porufication and waste removal are omitted from the price index used in wage bargaining.

16.   In the Netherlands the Water Boards are a prime example.

17.   This is the essence of the case made for earmarking by Buchanan (1963).

18.   To quote a political scientist: "... the significant choice is not among abstractly considered policy instruments but among institutionally determined ways of operating them" (Majone (1976)).

19.   Rees (1988), Hanley *et al.* (1990). In actual fact there may be good reasons for not putting "efficiency" first, as environmental policy processes the complicated constitutive issues of problem demarcation, scientific uncertainty, target setting and legitimacy building.

20.   Kelman (1981).

21.   Larrue (1991), discussing a case of water rate setting in the US. The political acceptability of the Dutch Water Pollution Charge has been attributed to its design as a user charge (Huppes and Kagan (1989)).

22.   Cf. also Majone (1976) and Hanley *et al.* (1990). Kelman (1981), discussing the political feasibility of economic incentives in environmental policy, stresses the need for an explicit *political* strategy, based on an analysis of the political process such as it really functions.

23.   Recently in the Netherlands this factor has prompted a more positive attitude of the Finance Ministry.

24.   Hanley *et al.*, p. 1435.

Bibliography

Bressers, J. Th. (1983): *Beleidseffektiviteit en Waterkwaliteitsbeleid*, Enschede 1983.

Buchanan, J.M. (1963): The Economics of Earmarked Taxes, *American Economic Review* 1963, 457-469.

Hanley, N., Hallett, S. and Moffatt, I. (1990): Why is more notice not taken of economists' prescriptions for the control of pollution?, *Environment and Planning A*, 1990, 1421-1439.

Hofstra, H.J. (1985): Het fiscale wetgevingsproces, *Weekblad voor Fiscaal Recht*, 1985/5672, p. 253-257.

Huppes, G. and Kagan, R. (1989): Market-Oriented Regulation of Environmental Problems in the Netherlands, *Law & Policy*, April 1989, 215-237.

Jansen, H.M.A. (1991): *West European Experiences with Environmental Funds*. Institute for Environmental Studies, Amsterdam, 1991 (unpublished).

Kelman, S. (1981): *What Price Incentives?*, New York 1981.

Larrue, C. (1991): *User charges and accountability: the Baltimore water utility*, unpublished paper.

Maathuis, H.H.M. (1990): Belastingen en Milieu. *Weekblad voor Fiscaal Recht* 1990/5915, p. 725-732.

Majone, G. (1976): Choice Among Policy Instruments for Pollution Control, *Policy Analysis*, Fall 1976, 589-613.

Mors, M. (1991): *A Survey of Recent CO_2 Tax Impact Studies*, Paper presented at BAEE seminar on CO_2-taxation, Den Haag 1991.

Opschoor, J.B., and Hans B. Vos (1989): *Economic Instruments for Environmental Protection*, OECD, Paris, 1989.

Rees, J. (1988): Pollution Control Objectives and the Regulatory Framework, in Turner, R.K. (ed.): *Sustainable Environmental Management: Principles and Practice*, Londen 1988, 170-189.

Rolph, E.S. (1983): Government Allocation of Property Rights: Who Gets What?, *Journal of Policy Analysis and Management*, Vol 3., 45-61.

Schuurman, J. (1988): *De prijs van water (een onderzoek naar de regulerende nevenwerking van de verontreinigingsheffing oppervlaktewateren)*, Gouda Quint BV, Arnhem, 1988 (with English summary).

Tietenberg, T. (1991): *Speech to the European Association of Environmental and Resource Economists*, Stockholm 1991.

in 't Veld, J. (1991): Road pricing: a logical failure, in Kraan, D.J., in 't Veld, J.: *Environmental Protection: Public or Private Choice*, Kluwer 1991.

VNG (Vereniging van Nederlandse Gemeenten, Association of Dutch Municipalities) (1990): *Gemeenten en afvalverwijdering*. The Hague, 1990.

VROM (1991): *Milieuprogramma 1992-95*, Ministry of Public Housing, Physicial Planning and Environment, Den Haag 1991.

Wasch, E.P.J. (ed.) (1990): *Hoofdzaken milieuheffingen* (Main issues regarding environmental charges), FED, Deventer, 1990.

Zeckhauser, R. (1984): Preferred Policies When There is a Concern for Probability of Adoption, *Journal of Environmental Economics and Management*, Vol. 8, 215-237.

ENVIRONMENT AND TAXATION:

THE CASE OF SWEDEN

(P. BOHM, Department of Economics, University of Stockholm)

Table of Contents

INTRODUCTION

Chapter 1 gives an overview of the main features of the Swedish tax system and economic instruments used for environmental policy. This is described in more detail in Chapter 2 along with some estimates of the revenue and environmental impacts of the taxes currently in use. Chapter 3 gives an overview of the recent policy debate concerning the tax system and the use of economic instruments in environmental policy. In Chapter 4, I comment on the Swedish tax system from the point of view of environmental policy. The main conclusions are presented in the final chapter.

A postscript is added to present the main contents of a bill that was proposed by the Swedish government in April 1992. If passed by the parliament, this bill will significantly change the structure of the environment related energy taxes in Sweden. The reader is advised to check the outline of the postscript before reading the report as a whole.

Chapter 1

OVERVIEW

Use of environmental taxes has remained a purely academic issue in Sweden until quite recently. For about 20 years, Swedish economists had been proposing economic instruments as the basic approach for efficient environmental policy and pointing out the important side effects of environmental charges or taxes in reducing the reliance on distortive taxes and hence in reducing the so-called excess burden of government revenue. Towards the end of the 1980's, this issue moved to the forefront of the political debate. Recently, it has significantly influenced practical policy in Sweden. The focal point of this policy change is the Swedish tax reform of 1991, where the introduction of a set of environmentally motivated taxes was given a significant role when the burden of indirect taxes was increased to allow for a reduction of direct taxes. It seems fair to say that, without the opportunity offered by the need felt to reduce income taxes while keeping the total tax volume intact, environmental taxes would not have been introduced to the extent that now is the case.

1.1   The 1991 tax -- and environmental policy -- reform

The main targets of the tax reform were to create a simpler and more "neutral" tax system and to diminish the perceived disincentives of the internationally speaking very high marginal income taxes in Sweden. To attain these targets, essentially the following changes were made:

a)   To avoid distorsions of consumer choice, the value-added (VAT) tax base for a uniform VAT tax was broadened.

b)   To reduce distorsions between labor and leisure, the marginal income tax rate was reduced to about 30 percent for some 80 - 90 percent of the income earners and to about 50 percent for the remaining high income earners (as compared to a top marginal tax rate of 73 percent in 1989 and 85 percent a few years earlier).

c)   To rectify the incentives for saving and borrowing, the capital income tax was made more uniform.

d)   To finance the reductions in income taxes, the VAT tax rate was increased and taxes on capital and energy were restructured and raised to higher average levels.

A third of the tax reform was undertaken in 1990, the rest in 1991. The change of the tax structure is shown in Table 1.1. The gross redistribution of the reform equals about 6 percent of GDP or 10 percent of total taxes (including social security contributions). The change in energy related taxes, which is in focus here, were expected provide an additional SEK 18,000 million, corresponding to somewhat more than about one percent of GDP or about two percent of government revenue in 1991/92. The energy related taxes were designed to meet certain environmental goals. (For a more comprehensive account of the tax reform, see "The Swedish Tax Reform of 1991", Ministry of Finance, Stockholm 1991.)

Table 1.1 **The Swedish tax structure for 1989 and 1991. Percentages of GDP**

	1989	**1991**
Direct taxes	25.3	21.3
Households	22.5	19.5
Corporations etc.	2.8	1.9
Indirect taxes excl.		
Social security contributions	14.7	16.9
Value added tax	7.6	9.8
Miscellaneous (excise duties etc.)	7.1	7.1
Social security contributions	16.5	17.8
Total taxes and contributions	56.4	56.0

Source: Ministry of Finance, 1991.

1.2 Overview of economic instruments in Swedish environmental policy

Prior to the changes now indicated, the instruments used for environmental policy were primarily of the command-and-control type. The subsidy systems for encouraging environmental improvements by industry and by local governments were essentially phased out during the 80's. Introduced before 1990, there are a number of indirect taxes which originally had a purely revenue-raising purpose, but which over time has been given the additional role of instruments for environmental policy. Various taxes on energy, in particular the general energy tax and the gasoline tax, can be referred to this category. If environment is defined in a very broad sense, part of the excise taxes on alcohol (concerning its effect on the social environment) and tobacco (deteriorating the air quality of nonsmokers) should perhaps also be included here.

Other taxes with a more specific purpose of environmental protection, existing before 1990 and still in use, are those on beverage containers (from 1973), fertilizers and pesticides (from 1984), mercury/nickel-cadmium batteries (from 1987) and NOx/HC emissions of domestic air transportation (from 1989). A tax differentiation between leaded and unleaded gasoline is in force since 1986. A set of administrative charges for registration, authorisation and control of various environmentally disturbing activities and products have been in use for some time. Non-compliance charges exist for proven violations of the Environment Protection Act (with small amounts so far collected) as well as for prohibited oil discharges from ships. Municipal user charges on water and waste are to a small extent used to reduce the volume of waste water and waste.[1] Deposit-refund systems have been employed to reclaim car hulks, beverage bottles, and aluminium cans. (See Table 1.2).

The environmental taxes introduced in connection with the tax reform in 1990-91 include a CO_2 tax on fossil fuel and a tax on sulphur in coal, oil and peat, both taking effect in 1991. In addition, the VAT has been extended to all fuels subject to energy taxation. At the same time the general energy tax was reduced by 50 percent. A charge on NOx emissions from large combustion plants will take effect in 1992. (See Table 1.2).

The expected total government revenue from taxes that can be related to environmental policy amounts to nearly SEK 50,000 million in 1992 or 3 percent of GDP (for details, see Chapter 2, in particular Table 2.6).

Table 1.2 Environment related taxes/charges in Sweden, 1992

Taxes/charges introduced prior to the 1991 tax reform:

General energy taxes
Gasoline taxes, diffentiated with respect to lead content
Vehicle tax
Kilometer tax (on diesel-driven automobiles)
Sales tax on new cars
Tax on domestic aviation
Nuclear power production tax and charge
Beverage container taxes
Charges on batteries
Charges on fertilizers, pesticides, herbicides
Administrative charges
Price control charge on agricultural products
(Alcohol and tobacco taxes)

Taxes/charges introduced in connection with the tax reform of 1991:

Carbon dioxide tax
Sulphur tax
VAT on energy
Nitrogen oxide charge

1.3   Main features of the Swedish tax system

As can be seen from Table 1.1, total taxes in Sweden in 1991 amount to 56 percent of GDP. About one third emanates from each of the three categories, income taxes (21.3 percent of

GDP), indirect taxes (16.9) and social security contributions (17.8). **Income taxes** derive primarily from personal incomes (19.5), all of which are subject to **local** income taxes at a rate of about 30 percent. Personal income below some SEK 200,000 is exempted from **national** income taxes. Above that limit, the national income tax rate is about 20 percent.

Social security contributions or payroll taxes, paid by employers and self-employed/non-employed, amount to about 40 percent of taxable personal income.

Indirect taxes, which are in focus here, consist primarily of the **value-added tax** (9.8 percent of GDP). The VAT rate of the tax reform was 25 percent, with few areas exempted from the tax. The idea of a uniform VAT rate was abandoned in late 1991. From January 1992, the rate is reduced to 18 percent for food and tourist-related services, primarily public transport, hotels and restaurants.

Other indirect taxes (7.1 percent of GDP) are first of all **excise taxes** on gasoline, other energy uses, alcoholic beverages, tobacco and motor vehicles. Including recurrent taxes on motor vehicles, the excise taxes amount to about 6 percent of GDP. **Customs and import duties** account for most of the remainder (0.8 percent).

Table 1.3 gives an overview of the Swedish tax revenues for 1989.

1.4   Current policy debate

The current policy trend related to the topic of this paper is towards further expanding the use of environmental taxes. The new right/center government as well as the Social Democratic government up to the elections in September 1991 have stressed the role of economic instruments in environmental policy. The revenue effect of a future expansion of environmental taxes or charges is likely to be quite limited, however.

In addition, various attempts will be made in the near future to adjust existing policy instruments to conform with EC rules. This may lead to a reduction in some of the environmental taxes and to abolishing some others (e.g., the system of sales tax differentiation of vehicles according to emission properties). Moreover, a special investigator appointed by the government has recently suggested that the total energy tax burden on industry should be lowered to EC levels, shifting the energy tax burden to non-industry energy users (see Chapter 3). Partly on the basis of this investigation, a government bill was presented in April 1992; the bill is still pending at the time of the writing of this report (see the postscript).

Table 1.3 The Swedish Tax Structure, details of tax revenue, in SEK millions, 1989

	1989
TOTAL TAX REVENUE	**686 450**
1000 Taxes on income, profits and capital gains	294 691
1100 Of Individuals	268 862
1110 On income and profits	267 234
Coupon tax	344
Duties on foreign artists	4
National income tax individual	77 577
Local income tax individual	191 247
Tax reduction individual	−1 938
Contribution national basic pension	–
1120 On capital gains	1 628
Lottery prize tax	1 628
1200 Corporate	25 829
1210 On profits	25 829
Tax on profits not distributed	79
National income tax B.C. list	23 040
Local income tax B.C. list	–
Special tax on profits	2 710
1220 On capital gains	–
1300 Unallocable between 1100 and 1200	–
2000 Social security contributions	179 647
2100 Employees	–
Health insurance fees	–
2200 Employers	170 714
National basic pension fees	49 922
Health insurance fees	51 536
Unemployment insurance fees	–
Labour market fees	5 486
Industrial injury insurance fees	3 909
Seamen's pension fees	21
Part pension fees	2 553
Supplementary pension fees	56 264
Wage guarantee fees	1 023
2300 Self-employed or non-employed	6 993
National basic pension fees	1 698
Health insurance fees	1 402
Industrial injury insurance fees	103
Part pension fees	90
Supplementary pension fees	3 700
2400 Unallocable between 2100, 2200 and 2300	1 940
3000 Taxes on payroll and workforce	22 411
Special employers fees	–
Child care fees	11 628
Adult education fees	1 379
Building research fees	–
Labour welfare fees	1 833
Labour education fees	–
Labour market fees	5 486
General wage fees	2 085
4000 Taxes on property	22 896
4100 Recurrent taxes on immovable property	6 362
4110 Households	2 711
Special tax on real estate	2 711
4120 Others	3 651
Forestry levy	378
Special tax on real estate	3 273

Table 1.3 (contd.) **The Swedish Tax Structure, details of tax revenue, in SEK millions, 1989**

	1989
4200 Recurrent taxes on net wealth	3873
4210 Individual	3798
4220 Corporate	75
4300 Estate, inheritance and gift taxes	1196
4310 Estate and inheritance taxes	901
4320 Gift taxes	295
4400 Taxes on financial and capital transactions	11465
Taxes on financial and capital transactions	5633
Turnovertax on securities	5832
4500 Non-recurrent taxes	–
4510 On net wealth	–
4520 Other non-recurrent	–
4600 Other recurrent taxes on property	–
5000 Taxes on goods and services	**165318**
5100 Taxes on production, sale, transfer, etc	159277
5110 General taxes	93279
5111 Value added taxes	93279
5112 Sales tax	–
5113 Other	–
5120 Taxes on specific goods and services	65998
5121 Excises	52923
Taxes on petrol and fuel	15817
Special sales tax	1140
Sales tax on motor vehicles	2432
Tobacco tax	5145
Tax on spirits	6087
Tax on wine	2649
Tax on beer and soft drinks	2308
Tax on energy consumption	15924
Taxes on electricity from certain sources	1026
Special sales tax motor fuel	–
Tax on cassette tapes	180
Tax on videorecorders	215
5122 Profits of fiscal monopolies	269
Alcohol monopoly wholesale	93
Alcohol monopoly retailing	176
5123 Customs and import duties	8185
Customs	2992
Agricultural levies	5193
5124 Taxes on exports	–
5125 Taxes on investment goods	–
Investment tax	–
5126 Taxes on specific services	4621
Betting tax	562
Advertisement tax	970
Tax on gambling	85
Other specific services	2587
Tax on charter travelling	417
5127 Other taxes on internat. trade and transactions	–
5128 Other taxes	–
5130 Unallocable between 5110 and 5120	–
5200 Taxes on use of goods and perform activities	6041
5210 Recurrent taxes	6041
5211 Paid by households: motor vehicles	1794
5212 Paid by others: motor vehicles	4173
5213 Paid in respect of other goods	74
5220 Non recurrent taxes	–
5300 Unallocable between 5100 and 5200	–

Source: OECD

Chapter 2

EXISTING TAXES AND THE ENVIRONMENT

The purpose of this chapter is to describe the existing fiscal instruments in Sweden to the extent they significantly influence environmental quality. In Section 2.1, those taxes and charges, at least partly designed for environmental-policy purposes, are presented along with an evaluation of their fiscal and environmental impacts. Section 2.2 tries to identify other taxes which would seem to have a significant environmental impact. The sources for the information provided here are, unless other sources are explicitly stated, based on data obtained from the Ministry of Finance.[2]

2.1 Taxes and charges related to environmental policy

2.1.1 Energy

General energy tax on fuels

The present general energy tax, in force since 1957, is levied on **oil, coal and gas**. Crude oil, waste oil, waste, biofuels and peat are exempted from this tax. The same is true for packages of oil with a maximum content of 5 liters.

There are a number of general deductions for excise taxes such as the general energy tax. All of these are straight-forward. Tax deductions specific for the general energy tax exist for fuels used in aircraft, rail and water transportation as well as for fuels used in electricity production or for purposes other than "energy production".

The present taxes are as shown in Table 2.1. The tax levels were reduced by 50 percent in January 1991.[3] This occurred when a CO_2 tax and a sulphur tax were introduced. The ambition here was that the reduction in the general energy tax would approximately compensate the group of energy users for the new taxes, while creating a substitution effect counteracting the use of fuels containing carbon and sulphur. The general energy tax for some of the petroleum products were reduced by an additional SEK 100 in January 1992. All three taxes mentioned are collected by the National Tax Board from those who produce taxable fuel in Sweden or use such fuel to produce an equivalent product and from those who import taxable fuel. Taxes on stored fuel can be postponed to the time when the fuel is consumed or sold to a party who is not tax liable. (For more details on the Govt bills of this and other energy related taxes, see "Economic Instruments in Sweden - with Emphasis on the Energy Sector", Ministry of the Environment, Stockholm 1991.)

Table 2.1 **General energy taxes on fuels, 1990 and 1992, SEK**

	1990	1992
Petroleum products (m^3) (1)		
Class 1 (urban-area diesel, etc.)	1080.0	90.0
Class 2 (normal light diesel, etc.)	1080.0	290.0
Class 3 (standard diesel, etc.)	1080.0	540.0
Natural gas (m^3)	0.35	0.175
LPG		
Motor gas (liter)	0.92	0.85
Other uses (ton)	210.0	105.0
Coal and coke (ton)	460.0	230.0

---

1.   Environmental classification of oils came into force in January 1991.
     The tax rates were then SEK 190 (class 1), SEK 390 (class 2), and
     SEK 540 (class 3). The energy tax on petroleum products belonging
     to classes 1 and 2 was reduced by SEK 100 in January 1992 in
     order to make these classes more attractive. At the same time, the
     definitions of classes 1 and 2 were upgraded.

VAT on energy

A value-added tax exists also for energy since March 1990. The rate is 25 percent of energy price including excise taxes. Fuels used in air transportation is exempted from VAT.
When it is said that taxes on energy were increased as a result of the tax reform, this is essentially due to the broadening of the value-added tax base now mentioned.

Carbon dioxide tax

The CO2 tax was introduced in January 1991. It is levied on **oil, coal, natural gas, liquified petroleum gas (LPG), gasoline and fuel for domestic airtransportation**. The tax base is calculated for the average carbon content and calorific values of the respective fuels.

The tax rate amounts to SEK 0.25 per kg of expected carbon dioxide emissions. The tax rates for the various fuels are as shown in Table 2.2. Tax deductions relevant for the CO2 tax are similar to those of the general energy tax. In contrast to the latter, fuel used for domestic air transportation is not exempted from the CO2 tax. (The structure of this tax is changed to a significant extent in a government bill, now pending, see the postscript.)

The obvious incentive here is to discourage the use of fuels which cause CO_2 emissions, the most important of the emissions of greenhouse gases. Since there is not yet any economically feasible method for trapping CO_2 emissions from fossil fuel combustion, fuel use is a simple and practical base for this tax. However, there is a rule allowing for a refund if fuels are shown to be used with no or reduced CO_2 emissions. Although not the reason for this exemption, the refund provides incentives for future development of less costly methods for trapping the CO_2 emissions.[4]

Sulphur tax

A sulphur tax was introduced to take effect in January 1991 and is levied on the sulphur content in oil, coal and peat.

Table 2.2 **CO_2 tax on fuels, 1992, SEK**

Oil (m^3)	720.0
Natural gas (m^3)	0.535
LPG	
Motor gas (m^3)	400.0
Other uses (ton)	750.0
Coal and coke (ton)	620.0
Gasoline and higher alcohols (m^3)	580.0
Aviation fuels, domestic transportation (ton)	790.0

The tax rate is SEK 27 per tenth of one percent (by weight) of sulphur content per m3 for **diesel fuel** and **heating oil. Coal, coke** and **peat** are taxed by SEK 30 per kg of sulphur. Specific deductions for the sulphur tax coincide with those mentioned for the general energy tax with the exception that fuels used for electricity production and rail transportation are not exempted from the sulphur tax (essentially only low-sulphur fuel is used here). There is no sulphur tax on oil with less than 0.1 percent sulphur. Thus, a sulphur tax is levied on fuels used for electricity production (with the purpose of encouraging the use of low-sulphur fuels).

To provide appropriate incentives the tax is refunded to those who have taken measures to reduce sulphur emissions from fuel use, in proportion to the estimated reduction obtained.

Gasoline and (m)ethanol taxes, kilometer taxes, vehicle taxes, automobile sales taxes, etc.

The tax on gasoline has been differentiated with respect to lead content since 1986. The rates since July 1st, 1991, are SEK 2.37 per liter unleaded gasoline and SEK 2.68 for leaded gasoline. The purpose of this differentiation is primarily to make car users shift to unleaded gasoline whenever feasible. This has met with limited success among those who can use both types, since many believe their engines perform less well with unleaded gasoline. However, the size of this group is diminishing since new cars have to be equipped with catalytic converters, hence requiring the use of unleaded gasoline.

The **tax on methanol and ethanol** is SEK 0.8 per liter. Unmixed ethanol used as engine fuel is to be excluded from this tax from January 1st 1992.

There is no tax on diesel-driven vehicles exactly similar to the fuel taxes now mentioned. Instead, there is a **kilometer tax** that varies essentially according to the type and weight of the vehicle. For example, the tax rates per kilometer are SEK 0.20 - 0.29 for most passenger cars, SEK 0.53 - 0.69 for trucks weighing 16 tons and SEK 0.40 for buses of the same weight.[5]

Especially after the tax reform, the basic principle of which meant that most indirect taxes other than a uniform VAT (now partly changed), environmental taxes and health-related taxes should be avoided, it would seem natural to include at least part of the **vehicle taxes and automobile sales taxes** among the energy-related and environment-related taxes. To that extent, they can be regarded as fixed taxes in a multi-part enviromental tax scheme for the use of automobiles. This is the reason for observing all of these taxes here instead of elsewhere in this report.

The annual **vehicle tax** varies according to type of vehicle, weight, number of axles and fuel type. The average tax is SEK 666 for passenger cars and SEK 4000 for trucks and buses.

The **sales tax** on new vehicles, so far levied according to weight, will be differentiated according to environmental qualities, beginning July 1st 1992 and starting with model year 1993. The vehicle tax in 1991 is SEK 6.40 per kg (with special rules for motorcycles) up to a weight of 3.5 tons. The revision of this tax is shown in Table 2.3. Class 1 refers to passenger cars, meeting the California requirements valid from 1994 (a SEK 4,000 tax subsidy), and heavy trucks and buses (above 3.5 tons) meeting more stringent limits on noise emissions as well as the EC requirements expected to be valid from 1996 (no tax change). Class 2 refers to passenger cars meeting the U.S. Federal requirements valid from 1994 (no tax change) and heavy trucks and buses meeting the EC requirement just mentioned, for which there will now be taxes as shown in the Table. Finally, class 3 includes other passenger cars (additional SEK 2,000 tax) and heavy trucks and buses meeting the Swedish requirements valid from the 1993 model year (taxes, see Table 2.3). The additional revenue of the taxes is expected to be neutralised by the sum of the tax subsidies and a reduction of the kilometer tax from January 1993. As already indicated, this tax/subsidy scheme has drawn criticism from the EC Commission for its potential effects as a trade barrier.

A scrapping charge exists since 1975 for all vehicles up to 3.5 tons, except motorcycles. From 1992, the rate is SEK 850. The revenue is transferred to a fund, which finances, among other things, a refund of SEK 1,500 (from January 1, 1992) to car owners leaving their car hulks to registered scrapping firms. These firms normally charge a fee for accepting the car hulks, so far often in the amount of the refund (SEK 500 during 1991), thus leaving a modest incentive effect.

It should be mentioned here that personal income taxation is adjusted to certain forms of car use. Although recently made much stricter, these rules still tend to support such use. The right to **private use of company cars** is subject to personal income tax. In 1991, the tax was raised from 22 percent to 35-42 percent of the purchase price of a new car, if the car is not more than three years old. Lower rates apply for older cars. In many cases, those who use company cars for private transportation do not pay for the use of gasoline; hence, there is hardly any incentive for them to limit the use of such cars. Employees using their own cars in their employment are allowed a deduction of SEK 1.20 per km. People using their cars to commute to and from work are a allowed a deduction (SEK 1.20 per km in 1991) if the distance and time saved exceed certain limits. In 1987, some 900,000 commuters were eligible for this deduction, resulting in the average actual gasoline price being some 16 percent below the market price (Carlen, Swedish Energy Board, 1991). The rates and rules have recently been made less favorable for commuters.[6]

Table 2.3 **Vehicle taxes according to emission classes, model year 1993 and onwards, valid from July 1, 1992**

	Passenger cars, light trucks		Heavy trucks, buses	
Original taxes	*SEK 6.40/kilogram*		*SEK 0*	
	Emission req's (gram/km)		**Emission req's (gram/kWh)**	
Class 1	NOx	.25	NOx	7.0
	HC (methane)	.25	HC	1.1
	HC (other)	.078	CO	4.0
	CO (running)	2.1	Particulates	.15
	CO (starting)	6.2		
	SEK 4 000 tax subsidy		*No change*	
Class 2	Nox	.25	As above	
	HC (methane)	.25		
	HC (other)	.16		
	CO	2.1		
	No change		*SEK 6 000 below 7 tons*	
			SEK 20 000 7 tons and above	
Class 3	Nox	.62	NOx	9
	HC	.25	HC	1.2
	CO	2.1	CO	4.9
			Particulates	.4
	SEK 2 000 add'l tax		*SEK 20 000 below 7 tons*	
			SEK 65 000 7 tons and above	

Source: Govt. bill 1990/91:156.

Charge on nitrogen oxide emissions

A charge on NOx emissions from **large combustion plants** took effect in January 1992. The charge corresponds to SEK 40 per kg of emitted NOx. Measurement equipment is installed in order to estimate actual emissions. Since this equipment is costly, the charge was limited to the (approx.) 200 furnaces and gasturbines that have an input of at least 10 MW and generate more than

50 GWh per year. To avoid discrimination against these plants, the revenues are redistributed to the charge liable group according to the amount of energy produced. This is, formally speaking, the first environmental charge system related to actual emissions, and, in addition, the first system, which compensates the group of charge payers for the income effect of a charge. However, in the latter respect, the CO_2 tax system can be said to use the same principle since the carbon content of fuels will in fact be released and energy users as a group were compensated for the CO_2 tax by a reduction in general energy taxes.

A special environmental tax on emissions of **hydrocarbons and nitrogen oxides,** levied on **domestic air transportation,** was introduced in 1989. The tax rate is SEK 12 per kg of HC and NOx. Thus, domestic air transportation is taxed for CO_2 as well as HC and NOx emissions.

Taxes on electric energy

Electricity is taxed in a differentiated manner. The rates are shown in Table 2.4. The **general electricity** tax (actually considered to be part of the general energy tax) is here seen to be differentiated between industrial and nonindustrial uses; in the latter case, the tax rate is lower for certain areas in Northern and North-western Sweden for reasons of regional policy.

The general energy tax and the CO_2 tax are deductable for electricity produced from fossil fuels.

There are additional electricity taxes on **nuclear power.** These are composed of a production tax in the amount of SEK 0.002 per kWh and a tax, formally regarded as a charge to be funded for the financing of final treatment of nuclear waste, in the amount of SEK 0.02 per kWh.

The additional tax on electricity produced in certain hydropower plants should hardly be mentioned as an environment-related tax. Its construction is such that it cannot be seen as related to any damage that may be related to the environment (e.g., scenic beauty). In fact, it can even be questioned whether it is appropriate to regard the general electricity tax as environment-related since it is levied also on hydropower.

Total tax levies on energy

The total tax levels per kWh for different types of energy, excluding the sulphur tax and the VAT, are shown in Table 2.5. The most important incentive effect of the restructuring of the energy tax system and in particular the sulphur and CO_2 taxes is probably that coal as well as LPG (for uses other than motor fuel) and natural gas have been made more expensive in relation

69

Table 2.4 General energy taxes on electricity, 1991, SEK per kWh

Industrial use (1)	.05
Non industrial use	
Certain Northern and North-western local councils (essentially regional support areas)	.022
Other areas	.072
Additional electricity taxes	
Nuclear plants (incl. the charge)	.022
(hydropower from large plants (2)	
Built before 1973	.02
Built 1973-1977	.01

---

1. Industrial use refers to firms whose primary electricity use is in Mining, Manufacturing and Electricity-Gas-Heating-Water Industry.

2. At least 1500 kW.

to oil. This is evident from the growth of total energy taxes on oil and coal since 1978, as shown on Figure 1. Taxes per kWh have been significantly smaller for coal than for oil, originally a result of policy adjustment to the oil crises in the 70's, but are now about the same. The Figure also shows the considerable adjustment of relative taxes made in 1991. In real terms, the oil taxes have now quadrupled since 1980, whereas the taxes on coal have increased about twentyfold.

Industrial energy use above a certain level is not subject to general energy taxes, CO_2 tax and electricity taxes. The total of these taxes are limited to 1.2 percent of the firm's sales value. For oil, however, only SEK 473 per m3 of the general energy and CO_2 taxes are included in the basis for calculating this total. This means that energy intensive industry, primarily cement, pulp and paper, iron and steel, chemical and mining, are protected from high tax burdens. For 1990/91, the revenue effect of the reduction was an estimated SEK 900 million (source: SOU 1991:90).

Commercial horticulture using energy to heat greenhouses does not have to pay general energy and CO_2 taxes in excess of 15 percent of the sum of these taxes. This reduction as well as that on industry is now reconsidered in connection with a possible reform of the energy tax burden for industry (see Chapter 3).

The general implications of the increased taxes on energy have been to promote energy saving in industry as well as in the household sector, e.g., by reducing the use of hot water, reducing indoor temperatures, and increasing insulation in buildings. The large increases in gasoline taxes and kilometer taxes have provided significant incentives to reducing car use and speed as well as shifting to new cars with higher mileage per liter and limiting the use of automobile equipment, which increases fuel consumption. To the extent that energy users regard these taxes on energy and gasoline as permanent in real terms, they also provide incentives for the development of new energy saving equipment and technology.

Table 2.5 **Excise taxes (excluding sulphur tax) on fuels, January 1992, SEK**

Fuel type/unit	General energy tax/ gasoline tax	CO_2 tax	Total excise taxes	
			SEK	SEK/kWh
Petroleum products (m3)				
- class 1	90.0	720.0	810.0	.089
- class 2	290.0	720.0	1010.0	.106
- class 3	540.0	720.0	1260.0	.12
Coal (ton)	230.0	620.0	850.0	.114
Natural gas (1000 m3)	175.0	535.0	710.0	.066
LPG				
- motor gas (liter)	0.85	0.40	1.25	.184
- other uses (ton	105.0	750.0	855.0	.067
Gasoline (liter)				
- unleaded	2.37	0.58	2.95	.339
- leaded	2.68	0.58	3.26	.362

2.1.2   *Other tax/charge bases*

Beverage containers

Early on, the problem of littering as well as the extra costs of waste treatment, when wastes are not sorted, contributed to retaining a tax on beverage containers. The rate is SEK 0.08 per **returnable glass or aluminium container**. For **disposable containers**, the tax rate is SEK 0.10 for 20 to 30 centiliters, SEK 0.15 for 31 to 70 centiliters, and SEK 0.25 for 71 to 300 centiliters. Paper and cardboard containers are excluded from the tax.

Figure 2.1   Energy taxes on oil and coal 1978-1991, nominal prices

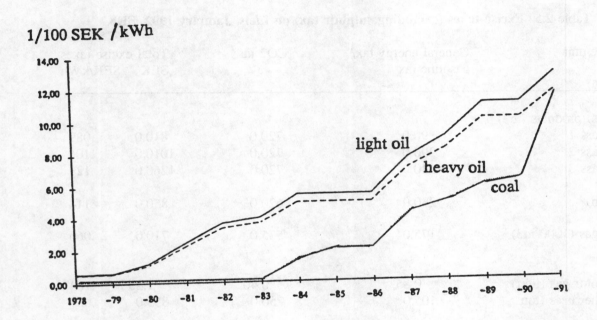

1/100 SEK /kWh

A deposit-refund system for **aluminium cans** is administered by a private company, which is required by government to provide a minimum return of 75 percent. The deposit is now SEK 0.50, giving a return rate of 85 percent.

Fertilizers and pesticides

Artificial fertilizers and pesticides used in agriculture are subject to a product charge since 1984. The rates on fertilizers are SEK 0.60 per kg of nitrogen and SEK 1.20 per kg of phosphorus. This represents about 10 percent of the present price of the most widely used types of fertilizers. The charge on pesticides is SEK 8 per kg of active substances, corresponding to about 5 percent of the present price level. The revenues from these charges are earmarked for environmental research, agricultural advisory service, counteracidification measures, etc.

Batteries

Since 1987, batteries are subject to a charge of SEK 23 per kg battery weight of **alkaline and mercury oxide batteries** and SEK 13 per kg battery weight of **nickel and cadmium batteries**. Batteries are exempted from the charges, if the total content of mercury oxides and cadmium is below .025 percent of the battery weight. This is now true for almost all alkaline batteries. There is a pending proposal to raise the charge on NiCa batteries from SEK 13 to SEK 300 per kg of battery weight and to introduce a deposit-refund system for these batteries some time during 1992.

Each lead battery weighing more than 3 kg is charged SEK 32 beginning 1991.

All these charges are earmarked for financing various activities to collect and process scrapped batteries. The charge levels were calculated so as to cover the costs of final disposal as well as the costs of information to the public of these charges.

2.1.3   Fiscal and environmental impacts

Estimated effects on emissions

The emissions reductions resulting from the restructuring of the energy tax system can be estimated only very approximately. Little time has passed since the tax reform and the changes or introduction of enviromental taxes took place. Hence, little can be said about the extent of the environmental effects. The only information available are the original estimates made by the government commissions proposing the environmental taxes/charges now introduced. Revisions of these now two to three year old estimates have not been made.

Carbon dioxide. Current CO_2 emissions are around 60 million tons. The Government's Environmental Charge Commission (ECC) estimated that, by the end of the 90's, the annual CO_2 emissions will be 5 to 10 million tons lower than they otherwise would have been, due to the new energy taxes including the CO_2 tax (see Govt bill 1990/91:90). The effect on coal use and thus, on CO_2 releases from coal, are likely to be considerable. There are reports indicating that individual local heating plants, possibly partly as a result of the tax change, are shifting from coal to biofuels. This shift is also supported by government subsidies available from July 1, 1991.

Sulphur. Another impression provided by the Swedish Industry Department is that there is a strong tendency for now some years, probably already in anticipation of the sulphur tax, to reduce the sulphur content in the fossil fuels used in Sweden. In 1990, the ECC estimated that, as a result of the taxes imposed, the total annual sulphur emissions of 110 kilotons in Sweden will be reduced by some 10 to 25 kilotons by the end of the century.

Nitrogen oxides. The ECC also estimated that annual NOx emissions (at a level of about 400 kilotons in 1991) will be reduced by some 3 to 5 kilotons below what they would otherwise had been at the end of the century, as a result of the measures taken (see Govt bill 1990/91:90). There is, however, complaints from the industry affected by the NOx tax that the lead time for taking actions has been too short in this case. Nevertheless, industrial and district heating plants are said to have taken steps to reduce emissions by several kilotons in anticipation of the tax taking effect.

Lead. The unleaded part of Swedish gasoline consumption is around 55 percent, at the end of 1991. The total gasoline consumption decreased during 1990 -- probably, at least to some extent as a result of the increased taxes on gasoline -- after having increased by 4-5 percent during the latter part of the 80's.

The ECC reported some broad qualitative estimates of the environmental implications of enviromental taxes and charge already in operation by January 1990 (SOU 1990:59, Appendix 3). For those taxes and charges still relevant at essentially the same levels in December 1991, not counting the effects from the earmarking of these for specific protective actions, the effect on the environment is estimated to be "low". This is true, in particular, for the charges on waste and waste water (local government), fertilizers and pesticides, beverage containers, batteries (prior to the pending changes), and all administrative charges. The effect of the deposit-refund system on car hulks is also estimated to have been small at the low refund levels prior to 1992. Thus, we may conclude that for the group of non-energy-related environmental charges or taxes the environmental effects are small.

As a result of the NOx/HC tax and the CO_2 tax, engines in airplanes used in domestic traffic have been redesigned and led to significant reduction of the emissions. Thus, for the Fokker F 28 planes, HC emissions are reduced by some 90 percent and CO_2 emissions by some 75 percent as compared to the period before these taxes were introduced (SOU 1990:59).

Estimated government revenue effects of environmental taxes and charges

The estimated revenues from environmental taxes and charges for fiscal year 1991/92 are shown in Table 2.6. The sum amounts to SEK 46,122 million, which omits revenue from some minor non-energy-related items and which uses data for 1988/89 in the case of non-energy-related items. Obviously, the revenue of approx. SEK 350 million (or no more than SEK 500 million) for these items represent at most one percent of the environmental taxes/charges and thus, an insignificant source of government revenue.

Taxes related to energy use provide almost all (99 percent) of the revenue from the environment-related taxes and charges. This corresponds to about ten percent of total central government taxes or 6 percent of total taxes in Sweden. These taxes (or total environment-related taxes) correspond to about 3 percent of GDP.

Of total taxes related to energy, 77 percent are general energy taxes (including also the general energy tax on electricity, SEK 6,228 million) and CO_2 taxes. CO_2 taxes alone account for 24 percent of the total. Taxes on vehicles and vehicle use represent 58 percent of the total. The gasoline and km taxes alone stand for 45 percent of the total.

As compared to the situation prior to the tax reform, there is now also tax receipts from VAT on energy. These additional receipts are estimated to be approx. SEK 3,500 million. Thus, total receipts from the environment-related taxes plus VAT on energy add up to approx SEK 50,000 million. As was mentioned earlier, these receipts were originally estimated to exceed by some SEK 18,000 million what would have been collected in the absence of the tax reform. Due to the slow-down of economic activity during 1990 and 1991, these additional receipts will be considerably smaller, perhaps only some SEK 14,000 million more. Still, the original figure is likely to be relevant for a non-recession period.

For international comparisons, the definition of environment related taxes/charges used here may be found to be too wide. As a minimum, Swedish environment taxes and charges would include the taxes on CO_2, sulphur, lead in gasoline (approx. SEK 1,000 million), NOx and HC in domestic air transportation as well as the non-energy related taxes or charges, in all a total of SEK 14,000 million, or 1 percent of GDP. Thus, the environmental taxes and charges in Sweden add up to an amount somewhere in the interval of 1 - 3 percent of GDP.

2.2   Other taxes

We have seen that energy-related or environment-related taxes amount to approx. 3 percent of GDP. As stated in Chapter 1, total taxes in Sweden correspond to 56 percent of GDP. The total of direct taxes, social security contributions (essentially a wage tax) and VAT stands for about 49 percentage points of that total. It is hardly meaningful to raise the question as to what the environmental impact of these taxes would be. Of course, comparing a set of such taxes with some other reference set, some environmental effects could be identified. However, the choice of a reference set is likely to be more or less arbitrary. Hence, we will not address any version of this general question here.

An exception should be made for special tax deduction rules and rules for the tax treatment of employment benefits to the extent that such rules seem to have an effect on the environment. The most important cases here are probably those concerning the deduction of certain expenditure for the use of private cars for commuting to and from work as well as those concerning the private use of company cars, etc. Information on this point was included in the preceding section (p. 15).

Another exception is the differentiation now introduced in the VAT system. From 1992, VAT on food as well as public transportation, hotels, restaurants and some additional services related to tourism is reduced to 18 percent from the otherwise uniform level of 25 percent. This reduction can be expected to have an effect on the environment, primarily to the extent that public transportation is substituted for car use. Part of the reason for the VAT differentiation was to support tourism in Sweden. If successful, this measure would lead to increased travelling and, if so, to additional emissions from personal transportation. Needless to say, no data are available on this point.

What remains to comment on then is the share of about 4 percent of GDP which various excise taxes other than those observed in the preceding section account for. Most of these taxes are listed in Table 2.7. Some of the excise taxes that exist now will be abolished as a part of the tax reform, while a second set of these taxes hardly can be expected to have any significant influence on the environment (see the Table).

What we are left with is a set of excise taxes with possible effects on the environment, but if so, probably not in conflict with environmental goals. As suggested earlier, taxes on alcohol and tobacco -- which internationally speaking are very high in Sweden -- may at the present time partly be explained by wishes to avoid the external effects of excessive consumption of such goods. However, this is not the place to speculate on the short-term or long-term effects on the social environment of these taxes.

The charter flight tax on international travel could be expected to have some effects on the volume of emissions from aviation in Sweden. However, the level of this tax (SEK 300 per person above 12 years of age) is small as a percentage of the average per-capita cost of such trips. Moreover, charter trips by bus have increased their share of the market, to some extent possibly as a result of the tax. In addition, if the tax has influenced consumer behavior, travelling within Sweden is likely to have increased as a result of the tax. Hence, the size as well as the sign of the environmental effect of the charter flight tax is uncertain.

Table 2.6 Estimated revenues for fiscal year 1992/93, SEK million

Total central government revenues		404 000
General energy tax		10 836
thereof on		
electricity	6 660	
fossil fuels	4 176	
CO2 tax		10 312
thereof on		
gasoline	3 287	
coal	1 958	
oil	4 779	
natural gas	159	
LPG	29	
Gasoline tax		14 413
Tax on electricity from hydroelectric plants		946
Tax on electricity from nuclear plants		141
Sulphur tax		552
NOx charge (1100, redistributed to the group of charge payers)		0
Tax on fuels used for domestic air transp.		170
Vehicle tax		4 100
Kilometer tax		3 235
Sales tax on new cars		1 660

Total taxes related to energy use (excl. VAT)		46 365
as percent of central govt. revenue	11	
as percent of total govt. revenue	6	
as percent of GDP	3	
Beverage containers (1988/89 acc. to ECC, App. 3)		115
Fertilizers and pesticides "		181
Batteries "		17
Administrative charges "		75
		————
Total environment related taxes/charges (excl. VAT)		46 753

(Estimated net contrib. from VAT on energy 1991-93 = SEK 3,500 million
 acc. to Govt. bill 1989/90:110)

Source: Ministry of Finance, April 1992

Table 2.7 Excise taxes on specific goods and services, excluding those related to the environment, 1990 (Source: National Tax Board)

Object of taxation	Revenues
1. Taxes to be abolished shortly:	
Cassette tapes	175
Chemico-technical commodities	494
Chocolate and confectionary	333
Soft drinks and mineral water (approx.)	200
Video tape recorders	188
2. Taxes without any obvious environmental effects:	
Public permits	243
General advertising	984
Gambling	703
Shares etc	7,358
3. Taxes with (at least potential) environmental effects:	
Charter flights	394
Spirits for consumption	6,205
Wine	2,922
Beer (approx.)	2,100
Tobacco	5,634

Chapter 3

THE POLICY DEBATE ON TAX INSTRUMENTS RELATED
TO ENVIRONMENTAL ISSUES

The purpose of this chapter is to review briefly the main issues of the current debate in Sweden as it relates to the use of environmental taxes. Only the author's personal perspective on this debate can be offered here.

As a general observation, it seems fair to say that both tax policy and environmental policy have been in focus for a considerable period of time. This is true for the parliamentary debate as well as the media debate. As one prime reason for this focus, it should be recalled that Sweden is a country of very high taxes (to finance its ambitious welfare policy). As another reason, it can be mentioned that Sweden traditionally has been environment conscious, regarding outdoor recreation as a essential part of consumer welfare.

The debate on tax policy as well as the use of economic instruments for environment policy escalated during the second part of the 80's. The need for a comprehensive tax reform and a more effective protection of the environment was highlighted in this debate. The latter point contributed to the emergence of a Swedish Green party, which in 1988 succeeded in being represented in Parliament for the first time. This position, however, was lost in the September 1991 elections, probably as a result of the combination of the following two factors. First, the traditional parties had now considerably increased their attention to environmental issues. Second, growth and employment problems now emerged as the dominating campaign issues.

Issues related to Sweden's application to join the European Community has also been in focus lately; the implications of EC membership for Swedish tax levels and tax design as well as for Swedish environmental policy have been among the central issues in this part of the debate.

In Section 3.1, an attempt is made to give a broad outline of the environmental-tax policy of the Swedish government, in power since the general elections in 1991. A sketch of the positions of the various political parties is presented in Section 3.2. Given the role of special-interest organizations in Swedish policy debate, an attempt to present the flavor of their positions is made in Section 3.3. Some of the proposals made by recent government commissions of inquiry, but so far not accepted by government, are presented in Section 3.4, along with brief account of some policy issues discussed by academic research in Sweden. The final section tries to indicate where Swedish tax and environmental policy is now headed.

3.1   Government policy proposals

A number of government proposals for introducing or expanding environmental taxes/charges were made and accepted by Parliament during the period 1989 to 1991. No equally important new proposals are expected for the near future. Instead, as already indicated, there is a distinct possibility that some of the environmental taxes now in existence may have to be redesigned and perhaps lowered as a result of the current and future Swedish attempts to adjust to EC rules. The concern over the - internationally speaking - high Swedish indirect taxes having an adverse effect on Swedish export is another possible reason for adjustment of the taxes discussed here.

The government environmental charge commission (ECC) has proposed a number of new taxes or charges in addition to those that have now been accepted in their essentials, the CO2 tax, the sulphur tax, the NOx tax, and the differentiated vehicle sales tax. For a review of the remaining proposals from this commission, see the summary of the commission's final report, reproduced in the appendix to this paper. A few comments on these proposals should be made here.

The tax on cadmium in fertilizers is under consideration and a proposal may appear during 1992. However, the prospects for it being accepted are small due to EC considerations. Environment-related landing charges for all air traffic in Sweden will probably not prove feasible. Thus, what will remain on this particular point are the taxes on domestic air traffic mentioned earlier. The other remaining proposals from this commission are unlikely to be accepted in the near future. But some of the proposed economic instruments have been replaced by regulations, e.g., on chlorinated solvents.

Since 1988, the Swedish government may allow the introduction of road user charges. Such charges will probably be introduced in the future, e.g., by the local governments in Stockholm and Gothenburg. Environmental considerations would probably play a role for this policy change, although fiscal reasons seem to dominate.

3.2   The position of individual political parties on tax and environment policy[7]

As far as environmental policy is concerned, the position of the present government, formed by four right-to-center parties, does not seem to differ a great deal from that of the Social Democratic party, the main opposition party and the former government party. Some difference on this point exists, however, among the present government parties.

The major government party, the Conservative Party (21.9 percent of the votes in the September 1991 elections), is the most conservative also in this respect, with an exception for its backing of higher CO2 taxes, replacing the existing energy taxes. The Center Party (8.5 percent) is generally regarded as the most environment conscious of the government parties; its leader is now Minister of the Environment and has been pressing, inter alia, for increased charges on unsorted waste. The Liberal Party (9.1 percent) has a middle position on environmental issues, but has been a leading proponent for high gasoline taxes and for the use of economic instruments in environmental policy in general. The position of the Christian Democrats (7.1 percent), first represented in Parliament in September 1991, seems close to that of the Center Party.

The Green Party (3.4 percent of the votes in the September 1991 election, but no longer represented in Parliament) and the Left Party (4.5 percent) have been regarded as the parties, along with the Center Party, most consistently emphasizing environmental issues. The Social Democrats (37.7 percent) were in power when the 1991 reforms of tax and environmental policy were carried out. Together with the Left Party, the Social Democrats are those most in favor of keeping the tax level intact. The Conservative Party has been the party most consistently stressing a need for lower taxes, joined by the Liberal Party, in particular, when advocating a redesign of the tax system. The new right-wing party, New Democracy (6.7 percent), is strongly in favor of lower taxes, with no detailed position on environmental policy as yet.

From an international perspective, it seems correct to say that there is a high degree of consensus among the political parties in Sweden regarding environmental policy and the use of economic instruments for this policy. There has also been wide agreement on the need for a tax reform, whereas the positions differ more significantly on the level of taxes. The political situation now described would seem to explain why it was at all possible for Sweden to arrive at such an extensive reform of the tax system and of environmental policy as that of 1990-91.

3.3   Large organizations

In Sweden, various "special-interest" organizations play a prominent role in the public debate, commissions of inquiry and sometimes also in the preparation of government policy decisions. The trade unions as well as the employers' federation have occupied the center stage of this debate on most of the policy issues. However, none of them, especially not the trade unions, have been very active concerning environmental policy. The employers' federation has, understandably for a high-tax country, been prominent in advocating lower taxes and a redesign of the tax system. It is true for a number of other large "special-interest" organizations that they off and on participate in the debates on taxes and environmental protection. To give a fairly complete coverage of the positions taken by such organizations in these respects might be appropriate for a country like Sweden, but would take us too far here.

Selecting a set of organizations for a presentation of their positions in this debate is obviously a delicate matter. There is, however, a possible defence for selecting only two of these organizations. The Federation of Swedish Industries has been prominent in the debate, representing interest groups which emphasize low tax burdens on industry and cautious environmental policy targets. In that capacity is also represents one camp of the policy debate under review here. As a representative from an opposite camp, it would seem appropriate to select the Swedish Society for Nature Conservation. This is the most prominent environmental organization in Sweden with a comprehensive approach to policy in most of the environmental policy issues.

Since the position of the Federation of Swedish Industries (SI) may be said to provide a lower bound -- in the Swedish power structure -- to what environmental policy should accomplish and to the use of environmental taxes and charges, it seems appropriate to give some details on its present stance in these matters. SI was up to recently in strong opposition to measures of environmental protection that would place a burden on Swedish industry. It had an outspoken negative attitude to, in particular, using economic instruments of environmental policy. In fact, industry and the Social Democratic government implicitly joined forces in combatting proposals to use environmental taxes. Both agreed, although for different reasons, to favor the use of direct regulations. Around 1985, after a period of almost complete regulatory dominance in environmental policy, economic instruments began to emerge as promising policy instruments also to politicians, in particular those from parties in the middle of the political spectrum. At about the same time, SI came out in favor of using such instruments, provided they were combined with certain policy adjustments (see below).

The present position of the SI is, according to the organization, well covered in an agreement among the sister organizations in the Nordic Countries (see Federation ..., 1990). Quoting from this agreement, the SI argues that local pollution from the industry is "for the most part under control. ... Global problems have to be solved globally." ... SI says "no to environmental charges which are introduced unilaterally ... in order to solve global environmental problems." The organization is "not opposed to the idea of ... environmental charges ... provided that:

-- such environmental charges, and other energy charges, do not ...exceed the level which applies in leading competitor countries...

-- charges /for global environmental problems/ are not introduced unilaterally ...

-- other taxes /are/ reduced accordingly. ...

-- charges are the most cost-effective means of achieving established environmental objectives, ..." and provided that

-- it is not the case that industry has "no alternative due to technical or practical limitations ... so that environmental charges lose their controlling effect and become a pure tax... This applies to a great extent to emissions of carbon dioxide..."

"Environmental charges should only be used in those cases where impact assessments show that they are better than administrative instruments from both the economic and environmental points of view."

The position of the other "extreme", represented by the Swedish Society for Nature Conservation (SNF), is essentially that of a traditional environmental organization with policy recommendations that go beyond those of the political parties on more or less all accounts. It is noteworthy, however, that SNF recently has been quite active in advocating the use of environmental charges and taxes. Thus, for example, the organization wants to go further than what was proposed by the ECC (see the Appendix), allowing fewer exemptions, e.g., for the NOx charge and the CO_2 tax, and advocating higher tax and charge levels, in particular a doubling of the present CO_2 tax. It is also noteworthy that the leading spokesmen for the SNF have been prominent members of the Conservative Party and the Social Democratic Party. The positions taken by the organization has, perhaps partly for this reason, been widely publicized in Sweden.

3.4   Commissions of inquiry and academic policy-related research

The 1989-90 reports from the government environmental charge commission (ECC) are still the dominating sources of specific proposals for new environmental charges and taxes in Sweden (see the Appendix). The reports are, however, conspicuous in not giving extensive attention to one of the most promising recent contributions to the arsenal of economic instruments for environmental policy, viz. the tradeable permit approach. In fact, the commission rejected the use of this approach without having made any detailed evaluation of its pros and cons. In particular, it payed little attention to the fact that this policy instrument is especially useful when the environmental targets are set (e.g., by international agreements) in terms of national emission levels, e.g., for CO_2, NOx and sulphur, and when it is of utmost importance (for a country that wishes to lead the way on transfrontier-pollution issues) that these targets are met. Using taxes or charges, whose emission elasticities are largely unknown, means either that the tax/charge level will have to be adjusted, perhaps quite frequently, to meet the targets more precisely, or that it will have to meet the target with a sufficient and hence, expensive margin.

The fact that the commission did not develop the tradeable-permit approach means that it did not present the politicians with the alternative to ordinary taxes/charges which, in addition to having the higher precision just mentioned, has the "same" government revenue potential as taxes or charges do. What is alluded to here is the version where tradeable permits are auctioned off by the government.

In Sweden, tradeable permits distributed by an auction mechanism have been suggested for CFCs (during the period up to a CFC phase-out) and CO_2, both of which provide ideal objects of application of the treadeable-permit approach due to the fact that the pollution effects here are independent of the location of emissions (Bohm, 1988, 1990a). The tradeable-permit approach has also been proposed on an experimental basis for 10-15 percent of CO_2 emissions, keeping the CO_2 tax for the remaining 85-90 percent, thus allowing for a comparative evaluation of the two approaches during a three-year period (Bohm, 1990a).

There has been considerable concern in Swedish industry over the effect of the high energy taxes on Swedish exports. A government-appointed special investigator recently published estimates indicating that the excess of Swedish energy taxes on industry over the tax levels of our main competitor countries has led to a loss of some 10 000 jobs, located especially in depressed regions (SOU 1991:90). In addition, there is the long-term risk that these taxes would make Swedish industry move abroad and/or have Swedish industrial output with its relatively low CO_2 emissions replaced by foreign production, which would tend to increase global GHG emissions.

The investigator proposes a radical reduction in total energy taxes on Swedish industry to approach the expected EC levels. Thus, oil taxes (class 3) would be reduced from SEK 1260 to SEK 130 per m3 with corresponding reductions for other fossil fuels, leading to an 80 percent reduction in total energy taxes for manufacturing industry but leaving NOx charges and sulphur taxes unchanged. In addition, present "limitation rules", in particular that relevant for energy intensive industry, limiting total energy, CO_2 and electricity taxes to a maximum of 1.2 percent of the sales value, should be abandoned to conform with GATT and EC rules.

In all, the proposed changes would reduce tax revenue by about SEK 4,000 million or 0.5 percent of total tax revenue. This reduction is proposed to be compensated by higher taxes on electricity and oil use by households and business other than industry, giving rise to two quite different price levels for fossil fuel.

The proposals are opposed, e.g., by environmental groups such as the SNF. An obvious drawback is that the differentiation of the user prices will promote inefficiency in fuel use and fuel savings and that significant incentives for black-market operations will be created. However, to reduce the tax burden on Swedish industry in other ways also has potential drawbacks with a possible exception for tax redistribution in relation to value added, e.g. administered within the VAT system. Another way to finance the tax reduction for industry than that suggested by the investigator, and a way that, under all circumstances, would limit the differentiation of tax-inclusive prices on oil would be to increase gasoline taxes (by some SEK 0.80 per liter).

3.5   The policy trend

Against this background, the question could be raised where Swedish tax policy in relation to environmental policy is heading. The present government as well as the preceding one have emphasized the role of environmental taxes. Some new taxes of this type can be expected in the near future. Their impact on government revenue is likely to be small, however.

Aside from adherence to GATT rules and the important constraints that EC rules impose on Sweden, if and when the country becomes an EC member, international constraints will probably have a small effect on the use of environmental taxes in Sweden. Even now EC rules and conditions influence Swedish policy in various ways. Environment-related taxes that are likely to be affected by such considerations in the near future are the differentiated vehicle sales tax, the kilometer tax -- both of which may have to go -- and the energy taxes on industry. As concerns the latter, the rules limiting the energy tax burden on industry will probably have to be abandoned. And -- for reasons of competition -- the internationally speaking very high energy tax levels may have to be reduced. (See Postscript).

Chapter 4

ASSESSMENT

In this chapter, some aspects of the scope (Section 4.1) and design (Section 4.2) of the environmental taxes presently in use in Sweden will be commented upon. The views expressed here are those of the author.

4.1   The scope for environmental taxation

As has been emphasized above, the present use of environmental taxes in Sweden and the effect of other taxes on the environment are dominated by what has happened during the years around 1990, when a significant reform of the tax system and of the instruments used for environmental policy took place.

An efficient tax system to finance a given set of government expenditures can be generally defined as one where the various tax instruments are used so that the costs in terms of the government objective function are minimized. Given that there are no sufficient lump-sum taxes to do the job, we end up with a complex tax design problem, which would be solvable if we had at our disposal a complete set of reliable data about the economy. Since this is not the case in actual fact, a set of basic guidelines for tax policy has been recognized as probably the best feasible and practicable choice. This set includes the idea of neutrality, according to which, among other things, commodity taxes should be uniform for an economy sufficiently close to being a perfect market economy. The Swedish tax reform of 1991 can be said to have tried to conform to this idea. However, given that the economy is not perfect, partly due to the existence of damaging environmental effects, it was recognized that an attempt should be made to let commodity taxes reflect such effects. In practice, this led to the introduction of a set of environmental taxes, to the extent transaction costs were not prohibitive, making total commodity taxes deviate from the structure of a uniform VAT system. This is at least how certain ambitions behind the reform can be described, ambitions that so far had not been present in Swedish policy.

Then, could the present Swedish tax and environmental policies be regarded as roughly efficient? Perhaps not. For one thing, there is still a number of special rules originating in special considerations to various industries (e.g. heavily energy-using industry) and households (e.g. certain car-using households). Now, it is conceivable to view these rules as ingredients of a system under transition, where it has been necessary to take into account what signals the previous system had provided for the long-term planning of producers and consumers. Thus, if additional information now were provided to the market indicating that the transition to an efficient tax system would be continued in the future, aiming at eliminating the remaining "distortions" and expanding the scope of environmental taxation, whenever called for by long-term efficiency considerations, it would still be possible to argue that the present system is close to being an optimal-feasible one. However, no clear information of this kind has so far been provided.

Nevertheless, it seems fair to say that important steps have been taken to expand the scope of environmental taxation towards a socially more efficient system for Sweden. This was accomplished by an extensive package deal involving adjustments of both taxes and environmental policy, which neutralized the otherwise so effective blocking power of special interest groups. Now, the future scope of environmental taxation is to a large extent determined by what is compatible with Swedish membership in the European community. But even without that constraint, it is not likely that environmental taxation in Sweden could be made much more comprehensive in the near future. Above, reference has been made to the policy menu of the proposals from the Environmental Charge Commission quoted in the Appendix. Some of these proposals do not appear to be politically acceptable on account of administrative considerations. But, whatever new environmental taxes will be introduced in the near future, they would seem to provide little additional government revenue. The major opportunities in that respect would seem to be to raise the tax levels for some of the existing taxes, primarily perhaps the gasoline tax. As we have indicated, some of the energy taxes may have to be reduced to prevent Swedish energy-intensive industry from moving abroad.

4.2 The design of environmental taxation

In this section, a set of issues is highlighted which concerns the design of environmental taxes and charges currently in use in Sweden.

Designing energy taxes as environmental taxes

As we have seen, energy taxes dominate among the taxes related to the environment. However, they are far from all being designed to conform with the environmental effects of different energy uses. Thus, for example, there are taxes on electricity, including certain "clean" forms of electricity such as hydropower, while fossil fuel taxes are deductible for electricity production (see Section 2.1.1). In order to make the energy tax structure as a whole more compatible with environmental policy targets regarding CO_2, sulphur and NO_x emissions, a more efficient design would be (a) to eliminate general energy taxes, including those on electricity, and raise the taxes related to these emissions and (b) to eliminate the deduction of fuel taxes in electricity production. As we indicated in the preceding chapter, there is in fact some political support for such a redesign of the tax structure, but so far it has been not effective.

Similarly, the limit to energy taxes on energy-intensive industry is in sharp conflict with efficient environmental policy. This limit implies that, if energy taxes exceed 1.7 percent of the sales value of a firm, the firm can increase its use of fuels without paying any additional energy taxes. Moreover, it means that the incentive for energy saving will differ among energy users and, in addition, is much less significant for energy-intensive industry than for small energy users, i.e., for those users who have a small capacity for energy saving. Although there may be reasons for keeping such rules over a limited period of time, it would seem overall efficient -- and contribute to stabilizing government revenue from this source -- if it were announced that this transition period will come to an end and, if so, if it were specified the date at which this will occur. (See Postscript).

Finally, it should be pointed out that the use of peat is excluded from the CO2 tax. Using peat as a fuel is not combined with any generation of new carbon sinks (which is true in practice for biofuels, also excluded from the CO2 tax). Thus, burning the peat instead of leaving it in the ground will, ceteris paribus, provide a net addition to CO2 emissions. For this reason, it seems that peat should be included among the fuels taxable under the CO2 tax scheme.

The use of inflexible environmental taxes under inflationary conditions.

In an economy threatened by inflation and especially with a rate of inflation exceeding that of its trade partners, government is often reluctant to "help" inflation by too readily adjusting to it. This is also true for Sweden. Thus, there has so far been weak political support for tax indexation, even when the objective of the taxes is to control pollution and the original tax schedule was carefully chosen to meet this objective. In addition, there has been a very low flexibility in adjusting the tax schedule, when inflation has in fact occurred and significantly reduced the real value of the taxes.

As an example of the implication of these circumstances, we can take the Swedish deposit-refund system for car hulks, which when introduced in 1975 was hailed as a case of effective use of economic instruments in environmental policy. The original refund of SEK 300 was not changed until 12 years later, when it had dropped to a real value of SEK 120 (in 1975 year's prices) and had lost most if not all of its impact.

Allowing inflation to arbitrarily set the level of the real value of taxes and charges obviously threatens the effectiveness of the present system of economic incentives, a fact stressed e.g. by the Swedish Society for Nature Conservation. The increased reliance on environmental taxes makes the efficiency of Swedish environmental policy particularly vulnerable to imperfections of this type.[8]

Redistribution of tax proceeds to neutralize average income effects of environmental taxes.

A number of factors makes the use of an environmental tax contingent upon the introduction of some compensation to the (group of) tax payers in question. One reason is of course "purely political"; another is that the tax otherwise would distort competition within the country or internationally. Such a policy of redistribution can appear to be rather sophisticated and therefore easily misunderstood by politicians or media, as the Swedish debate has shown. It requires an understanding of the phenomena economists call income and substitution effects. Nevertheless, Sweden has used this approach on two occasions, one related primarily to avoiding distortions of domestic competition, the NOx tax on large combustion plants, and the other related primarily to international competition, the reduction in general energy taxes when the CO2 tax was introduced (see Section 2.1.1).

As mentioned in Section 3.4, it has now been proposed that energy taxes for industry should be reduced to avoid discrimination against Swedish industry on the world market and/or to discourage emigration of Swedish energy-intensive industry. Focussing on the CO_2 tax as an instrument to reduce CO_2 emissions, the argument was made that this global environment issue should be solved by international policy. However, the Swedish government may be said to have taken the step to a high level of energy taxes, a significant part of which is CO_2 taxes, in order to show its willingness to make sacrifices for the global common good, thus hoping to set an example for others to follow. Backing from this position and reducing the level of energy taxes for industry, regardless of whether this is said to be a reduction of the CO_2 tax part or the remaining general energy tax part, Sweden would obviously no longer be able to influence international greenhouse gas policy. As suggested earlier, a possible alternative could be to retain the present level of energy taxes for industry but reduce the income effect of these taxes by redistributing the energy tax receipts in some other way, e.g., in relation to its value added.

The use of "multi-part" environmental taxes.

A considerable part of environment-related taxes in Sweden concern the use of energy for transportation. A policy ambition exists -- insufficient according to many observers -- to set taxes on street and highway traffic according to total social costs, including environmental effects, but an ideal differentiation of user charges is considered practically impossible. Instead, the present tax system is designed as a multi-part scheme with sales taxes on new cars, annual taxes on cars in use, and gasoline taxes or kilometer taxes roughly according to use. If the use-related part is deemed suboptimal on the average, as some contend is still the case in Sweden, this is hardly an efficient arrangement. If so, there are environmental arguments for transferring a share of the "fixed" charges (the sales and the vehicle taxes) to the variable part of the tax system. In the opposite case, where use-related charges tend to be superoptimal, a case likely to be relevant at least if and when toll systems will be introduced in the largest cities, a shift in the reverse direction might be called for.[9] Such marginal adjustments of the tax structure is, of course, not prohibited by practical considerations.

Concentrating on the two "fixed" parts of the tax scheme, the sales tax and the annual vehicle tax, the distribution between them may not be the ideal one. The higher the sales tax on new cars or trucks, the higher the incentive to keep old vehicles going, i.e., those with the poorest performance from an environmental point of view. Whatever the special sales tax is accomplishing, it could go on doing that, given a reasonably perfect credit market, if installments of that tax is transferred to the annual tax, thus eliminating the incentive of the sales tax to keep old and heavily polluting vehicles in use. The Swedish tax system for vehicles is unlikely to be efficient at least for this reason.

The use of earmarking of environmental taxes and charges

Most of what is formally called environmental charges in Sweden is earmarked for specific uses of the revenue obtained. As indicated in Chapter 2, the sums involved are small. Moreover, earmarking may be defended even from an efficiency point of view if charges otherwise would not be politically acceptable. This is particularly true when the activities financed in this fashion are such that they would have been carried out by the government even without this specific source of funds. This is also likely to be true for most of these earmarked funds in Sweden.

Now, when environmental taxes have been introduced on a large scale, earmarking would be more likely to cause efficiency problems as regards either the volume of the particular government expenditure or the level of the tax rates or both. It is therefore important to note that the environmental taxes now introduced in Sweden have not been earmarked.

The inefficient design of non-compliance charges

Although, strictly speaking, neither a tax nor a charge, the system of charges imposed on parties proven not to be in compliance with the Environment Protection Act should be briefly commented on. Few violators of this Act have been brought to court and even fewer have been sentenced to pay the fines that this non-compliance charge amounts to. The burden of proof is heavily placed on the prosecutor, who has to (a) identify the person in the company who was responsible for the damaging emissions and (b) establish how much the company actually gained from this violation of the Act. The reason for this last point is that the charge is limited to the amount of that gain.

This is one of the first economic instruments used by the Swedish government for environmental policy. It was designed during a period when economic reasoning obviously had little influence: The significant prosecution costs per case were covered by the tax payers regardless of the outcome; the incentive effect on the violating person or firm was limited to the stigmatisation effect of getting caught, which was highly unlikely; the economic incentive effect was obviously perverse, since the detection risk was well below one and therefore the expected gain from violations of the Act well above zero. The total incentive effect is at best uncertain, whereas the revenue effect on the government is clearly negative.

Tradeable permits vs traditional taxes.

Sweden has so far chosen not to use tradeable permits with an auctioning of permits, providing the same amount of government revenue as would a tax with the same effect on emissions. With the use of an auction mechanism, a tradeable-permit system amounts to a system of (endogenous) taxes. In fact, the government has abstained from carefully investigating the potential use of this instrument even for cases where it is a promising candidate for efficient policy. Such cases are e.g. those where the environmental effects are independent of the location of the emissions and where ascertaining the attainment of a specific level of emissions is important. As mentioned in Section 3.4, these conditions are met for global pollution problems connected with CFC emissions and CO_2 emissions.

Chapter 5

MAIN CONCLUSIONS

There has recently been a more or less general political agreement in Sweden to extend significantly the use of taxes and other economic instruments for environmental policy. Most of the Swedish excise taxes, now in existence, can be seen to be roughly compatible with environmental policy objectives. No excise tax has been found here that is in obvious contradiction to these objectives.

The Swedish tax reform of 1991 amounted to an increase in indirect taxes in order to reduce direct taxes. As part of this reform, environmental taxes were given a prominent role, providing an additional 2 percent of total government revenue. The perceived need to reduce direct taxes in Sweden offered an opportunity to introduce environmental taxes to an extent that otherwise probably would not have been possible.

Using a narrow definition of environmental taxes, total government revenue from this source is at least 1 percent of GDP. However, counting all taxes and charges that can reasonably be related to environmental policy, they amount to 3 percent of GDP (or nearly SEK 50,000 million in 1992).

The present government as well as the preceding one have emphasized the role of environmental taxes. Some new taxes of this type can be expected in the near future, but their impact on government revenue is likely to be small.

EC rules will influence, and possibly reduce, the level of environmental taxation in Sweden. Taxes that are likely to be affected by such considerations in the near future are the differentiated vehicle sales tax and the kilometer tax, both of which may have to go.

The new taxes on CO_2 and sulphur are levied on the carbon and sulphur contents of fossil fuels. Since these taxes are refundable, to the extent that CO_2 and SO_2 emissions are shown to be avoided, these taxes will emerge as approximations to a charge on emissions.

The design of the present environmental taxes has been commented upon in the preceding chapter. In particular, it was noted that:

-- there do not seem to be any strong reasons, at least not after a period of transition, against redesigning energy taxes to conform better to existing environmental policy goals;

91

-- in the absence of an indexation of the tax rates, the efficiency of Swedish environmental taxes is jeopardized by inflation;

-- the introduction of redistribution or compensation arrangements have mad possible an extended use of environmental taxes in Sweden; such arrangements for neutralizing the income effects of environmental taxes would need to be used also for protecting Swedish industry from the effects of the present high level of energy taxes, which otherwise may have to be reduced;

-- vehicle sales taxes are counterproductive from the point of view of environmental protection and should probably be replaced by increased annual vehicle taxes;

-- tradeable permits (auctioned off by government to provide the same revenue as traditional taxes do) have not yet been seriously considered for practical policy in Sweden, even for cases where this policy may well be the most efficient option.

Notes

1. User charges are not included in the subsequent review of environment related taxes in Sweden. The review covers all taxes and charges, not paying any systematic attention to the formal, and from an analytical point of view more or less arbitrary, distinction between the two terms.

2. Special thanks are due to Ms Marianne Svanberg from the Ministry of Finance for her help in providing and checking the data as they are presented here.

3. The reduction of the energy tax on motorgas was limited to SEK 0.07 per liter.

4. This contrasts favorably to the practice used by the Montreal Protocol on CFCs, another global pollutant, where a recovery of CFCs cannot generally be netted from CFC use, only from CFC production (see Bohm 1990).

5. The CO_2 tax per liter is SEK 0.58 for gasoline, SEK 0.72 for diesel and SEK 0.40 for LPG.

6. Available estimates indicate that abolishing this deduction altogether, long-term gasoline consumption would be about 3 percent below the level relevant for the rules existing in 1987 (Carlen, op.cit.).

7. This section relies heavily on a study of the environmental-policy positions of the political parties in Sweden, conducted by the Swedish Society for Nature Conservation, 1991.

8. It should be noted that, when tradeable permits are used, inflation will no longer be a problem since the "taxes" here are endogenously determined to make the system attain the given emission targets.

9. There exist elaborate plans to introduce tolls on automobile traffic in Gothenburg and Stockholm.

Postscript

In April 1992, the Swedish government presented a bill which -- if accepted by parliament (the bill is still pending at the time of writing) -- would significantly change the Swedish tax system as it relates to energy use and the environment. The background to the proposal is given by (a) the need to deal with the energy tax limits for industry, which may be found to be incompatible with GATT principles and EG rules, and (b) the need felt to reduce the heavy tax burden on energy use in the Swedish industry as compared to its competitors. Both points were noted above.

The pending government bill includes the following points, relevant to observe in the present context:

1) The tax limits on energy taxes effective for energy intensive industry and commercial horticulture will be abolished by January 1993. However, as a temporary arrangement during 1993 - 1994, the CO2 tax payments will be limited for industry. (SNI code 2 and 3) to 2 percent of the firm's sales value (now 1.2 percent). (Refers to p. 19 above.)

2) The general energy tax on fuels and electricity will be eliminated for industry and commercial horticulture from January 1, 1993. (Refers to pp. 10 and 17.)

3) The CO_2 tax for industry and commercial horticulture will be reduced from SEK 0.25 to SEK 0.08 per kg CO2 from January 1, 1993. The new level of this tax corresponds to a tax on oil of about USD 5 per barrel. (Refers to p. 12.)

4) The CO_2 tax for other energy users will be raised from SEK 0.25 to SEK 0.32 per kg CO2 by January 1, 1993. (Refers to p. 12.)

5) The general energy tax on electricity for energy users outside industry and commercial horticulture will be raised by SEK 0.013 per kWh from January 1, 1993. (Refers to p. 17.)

The revenue effect of the energy tax reductions is more than balanced by the energy tax increases now mentioned. The estimated net increase in government revenue is SEK 610 million. It may be noted that, according to the bill, the VAT tax rate of 25 percent will be reduced to 22 percent. Furthermore, income tax deductions for costs for commuting to and from work will be eliminated for the first SEK 4,000, which to some extent may discourage the use of automobiles for commuter trips (see p. 15 above). Finally, the increase of the CO2 tax on diesel fuel will be compensated for by a reduction of the kilometer tax for heavy vehicles (see p. 14).

Two aspects of the proposed energy tax changes should be highlighted here. The proposed changes imply that:

a) A significant differentiation of both the general energy tax and the CO2 tax would be introduced between industry and non-industry energy users;

b) The tax differentiation between heavy energy users and others, caused by the tax limits that now exists, would be reduced by 1993 and fully eliminated by 1995.

Annex I

SUMMARY OF THE PROPOSALS OF THE GOVERNMENT'S ENVIRONMENTAL CHARGE COMMISSION

Transport

The ECC proposes a system of <u>environment-related landing charges</u>, to be determined on the basis of international certification data for civil aircraft engines. In estimating these charges, hydrocarbons and nitrogen oxides have been valued at 25 Swedish kronor (SEK)/kg and carbon dioxide at 25 bre (SEK 0.25)/kg. The system of charges also covers noise. Before the proposal is implemented, further analyses of the limitations imposed by international agreements may prove necessary.

The ECC proposes that a <u>system of charges for shipping</u>, aimed at reducing discharges of sulphur in proximity to Sweden, be introduced. The proposal is based on the assumption that it is impossible, in the near future, to achieve international agreements to impose direct regulations to reduce sulphur discharges from shipping. The sulphur charge is based on the extra cost, for various types of vessels, of using low-sulphur oil. The proposed system includes both domestic and foreign shipping. Nevertheless, here too international negotiations are required before the system can be introduced.

The ECC proposes that the <u>sales tax on motor vehicles</u> levied on all new vehicles be supplemented by a special tax on passenger cars which, in mixed driving conditions, consume more than 0.9 litres of petrol per 10 km. For consumption of between 0.9 and 0.95 l per 10 km, SEK 300 of tax is payable for each 1/100 l per 10 km; thereafter, the amount charged is raised to SEK 400 for each 1/100 l per 10 km up to and including 1.05 l per 10 km. For each additional 1/100 l per 10 km, SEK 500 is to be charged, subject to a maximum of SEK 20,000 altogether per car. At the same time, the ECC proposes to lower the present sales tax of SEK 6:40 per kg of service weight by 10 re per kg for passenger cars in order for the total tax levied on all new passenger cars to remain unchanged.

The ECC also proposes to supplement sales tax by a tax on cars with high-powered engines in relation to their weight. A tax of this kind primarily affects sports cars and GTI models. The proposed tax is SEK 600 for each kilowatt by which the ratio of engine power to service weight exceeds 80 kW per 1,000 kg of service weight.

The date on which it is proposed that these changes in sales tax should come into force is 1 July 1992.

Cadmium in batteries

Cadmium in rechargeable nickel/cadmium batteries now accounts for more than half of all cadmium used. The ECC proposes that sealed nickel/cadmium batteries should be subject to a charge of SEK 0:50 per gram of battery weight. These charges should be introduced on 1 January 1992 and, with effect from 1995, be raised to SEK 1:00 per gram. To encourage consumers to return used nickel/cadmium batteries and appliances, returnable deposits should be payable from 1992 onwards. These batteries are used in, for example, gardening equipment and cordless telephones.

Wood-impregnation chemicals

The amount of arsenic used for wood impregnation in Sweden considerably exceeds the total amount discharged from Swedish industry. The ECC proposes a charge of SEK 200 per kg of arsenic and SEK 100 per kg of chromium in wood-impregnation preparations, with effect from 1 January 1992.

Chlorinated solvents

The use of chlorinated solvents in such industries as engineering and pharmaceuticals, and in dry-cleaning establishments, entails major risks to the environment and human health. The ECC therefore proposes that a charge of SEK 50 per kg of methylene chloride (dichloromethane), perchloroethylene (tetrachloroethylene) and trichloroethylene be introduced. To give users a chance to adapt, the ECC proposes that the charge be introduced on 1 January 1993.

HCFC compounds

The ECC report describes a system of environmental charges on HCFC compounds. Nevertheless, the ECC believes that this proposal cannot be implemented until the question of substances to replace CFC compounds (freons) has been tackled within the framework of the Montreal Protocol.

Agriculture

The ECC proposes that the environmental charge on nitrogen in artificial fertilisers be raised to SEK 2 per kg of nitrogen. The charge should also apply to fertilisers used in forestry, horticulture and other sectors. The proposed date of introduction of the charge is 1 July 1991.

The ECC proposes that the environmental charge on Phosphorus in fertilisers be retained, for the time being, at its present level, i.e. SEK 1:20 per kg of Phosphorus. This charge should be reviewed in conjunction with the introduction of a charge on cadmium in phosphorous fertilisers.

The ECC recommends that a charge on cadmium in fertilisers be introduced as an incentive to reduce the cadmium content to less than 5 grams per tonne of phosphorus. The cadmium charge is to be introduced only after a period sufficiently long to permit manufacturers to install equipment for cadmium removal, or to take other measures to cut cadmium use radically. This adaptation process should be completed by 1993.

The ECC considers that the environmental charge should be reconstructed for the pesticides that are currently subject to both the price-regulation and the environmental charge. The charge should be related to the ascertained dose per hectare for the pesticide concerned. The ECC proposes that this charge should, during a transitional period, be set at SEK 40 per dose. The charge covers all use of these pesticides, i.e. including their use in forestry, horticulture and other sectors. For the pesticides that cannot be included in the system of dose charges, the ECC proposes that the current system and level of charges, i.e. SEK 8 per kg of active substance, be retained for the time being. The proposed date on which the new charges would come into force is 1 July 1991.

Moreover, the ECC proposes that the Swedish Chemical Inspectorate be charged with the task of devising a detailed basic proposal for differentiated charges according to the hazardousness of different pesticides. A system of charges along these lines should come into force in 1995 at the latest.

The ECC has also elucidated issues relating to environmental charges on bare arable land, ammonia emissions from farmyard manure and cereal-growth regulators. It proposes that the authorities concerned carry on their work on these instruments.

Waste

The ECC proposes that a charge be imposed on unsorted household and industrial waste, with effect from 1 January 1992. The initial charge should be SEK 50 per tonne of waste. An increase in charges is proposed with effect from 1994. The ECC recommends that deductions be permitted for sorted components, such as glass and paper used in recycling of materials, clean wood for incineration and clean compost.

Certain types of "sector-specific" waste, from such sectors as mining, pulp and paper production and from being levied only on discharges exceeding the level of 0.5 kg of chlororganic substance (in terms of adsorbable organic halogen, AOX) per tonne of pulp.

Two new environmental funds

To consolidate environmental work, the ECC proposes the formation of two new funds: the waste fund and the chemicals fund. The waste charge will, as we have seen above, be paid into the waste fund. The chemicals fund will, according to the ECC's proposals, receive the proceeds of the charges on arsenic, chromium, chlorinated solvents and chlororganic substances, as well as the net proceeds from the charge on cadmium in batteries. The chemical fund should be used primarily to accelerate the phasing-out of hazardous substances. The two funds will, in the first two-year period, have at their disposal a total of SEK 1 billion.

Bibliography

BOHM, Peter (1988), "Economic Instruments for Reducing CFC Emissions", Nordic Council of Ministers, Copenhagen

BOHM, Peter(1990a), "Tradeable Permits for CO2 Emissions" (in Swedish), Swedish Energy Board, Stockholm 1990a

BOHM, Peter (1990), "Efficiency Issues and the Montreal Protocol on CFCs, Environment", Working Paper no. 40, World Bank, Washington, D.C. 1990

CARLEN, Björn (1991), "The Effects of Taxation Rules on Car Use"(in Swedish), Swedish Energy Board, Stockholm

Federation of Swedish Industries (9 May, 1990), et al., "Charges in International Environmental Work -- the View of Nordic Industry,"

Ministry of the Enviroment (1991), "Economic Instruments in Sweden-- with Emphasis on the Energy Sector", Stockholm 1991

Ministry of Finance (1991), "The Swedish Tax Reform of 1991", Stockholm

National Tax Board (1991), "Fact Sheet on Swedish Excise Taxes" (in Swedish), Ludvika 1991

SOU 1990:59, "Final Report of the Government's Environmental Charge Commission, (ECC)"

SOU 1991:90, "Neutral Energy Taxation" (in Swedish with summary in English), Government Commission Report

ENVIRONMENT AND TAXATION:

THE CASE OF THE UNITED STATES

(W. E. OATES, Department of Economics, University of Maryland and University Fellow, Resources for the Future)

Table of Contents

INTRODUCTION

The impact of taxation on the environment in the United States has consisted primarily of the side effects of taxes that were designed and introduced with other objectives in mind. This does not mean, however, that the subject of "pollution taxes" has been entirely ignored. As early as 1971 a bill was introduced in the U.S. Congress for a nationwide tax on sulfur emissions into the atmosphere. And again, more recently in 1987, a bill in the House Ways and Means Committee proposed national taxes on sulfur and nitrogen oxide emissions.[1] While such bills have not come close to enactment, they do indicate the presence of some interest in such measures.

Moreover, the current policy "atmosphere" is, in certain important ways, more receptive to proposals for pollution taxes than in past periods. First, the prevailing sentiment is strongly oriented toward market measures for the solution of social problems. There is a widespread sense that coercive public regulations of the CAC variety have not proved fully effective in achieving our economic, social, and environmental objectives. The current emphasis is on "incentive-based" measures that provide market signals to individuals to behave in socially beneficent ways (Hahn and Stavins, 1991). And this represents a major departure from earlier policy stances. President Bush has made this quite explicit. In discussing potential policies for addressing the problem of global climate change, the President asserted that "Wherever possible, we believe that market mechanisms should be applied and that our policies must be consistent with economic growth and free-market principles in all countries" (Hahn and Stavins, p. 3). Second, these are times in the U.S. of extreme budgetary stringency. The huge deficits in the federal budget have sent policy makers searching for new sources of revenues. Indeed, the proposed pollution tax legislation in 1987 had, as much of its motivating force, its potential as a revenue source. In the current setting, proposals for environmental taxes are likely to receive a more sympathetic hearing than in the past. There is, for example, serious ongoing discussion of systems of taxes to discourage carbon emissions into the atmosphere as a means of addressing the threat of global warming.[2]

The purpose of this report is to provide both a description and assessment of the impact of the system of taxation in the United States on the environment. I begin in the first section with an overview that provides a conceptual framework for thinking about the role of taxes and the environment. My purpose here is to review briefly the theory of pollution taxes both as instruments for environmental management and as potential sources of revenue--and the potential conflicts that such dual objectives can pose in the policy arena. Section II then turns explicitly to the structure of taxes in the United States and explores the way in which various tax instruments impinge (positively or negatively) on environmental quality. Section III proceeds to the current policy debate on tax measures for environmental protection. And the concluding section provides an assessment of the potential of tax policies for addressing our environmental problems and some thoughts on their design and implementation.

Chapter 1

OVERVIEW

1.1   Some theoretical background

The economic theory of environmental regulation sets forth in rigorous terms an explicit role for taxes on polluting activities. Pollution, from this perspective, is seen as a side effect of production and consumption in the economy: this side effect (or "externality") is a form of social cost that is not borne by the agent who is its source. The theoretical analysis leads to a straightforward prescription to correct the misallocation of resources that results from these side effects on the environment: a unit tax on the polluting activity that is equal to the marginal social damage of the pollution. Such a Pigouvian tax has the potential to "internalize" the external cost and can lead to socially efficient levels of environmental protection. The nature and properties of such taxes on pollution have been worked out carefully in the literature in environmental economics (see, for example, Baumol and Oates, 1988).

Such taxes will also, of course, be the source of public revenues. And this has received somewhat less attention in the literature. However, it is a straightforward matter in principle to extend the analysis of pollution taxes to take account of their role as a source of public revenues as well as an instrument of environmental management (Lee and Misiolek, 1986; Oates, forthcoming). We turn to this issue now.

From the revenue perspective, pollution taxes are seen as a subset of potential revenue instruments. In an optimal-taxation framework, the basic objective is to design a system of taxation that generates the requisite revenues at the least cost to society. The problem here is that most conventional taxes have distorting side effects on the functioning of the economy: in the course of producing revenues, they introduce distorting incentives for individual economic behavior such that the full cost of the taxes to society exceeds the level of the tax revenues that they produce. An efficient tax system will minimize these additional costs (the so-called "excess burden") from taxation. This requires, in principle, that the rates on the various tax bases be set such that the excess burden from an additional dollar of revenue is equated across all revenue sources (e.g., Rosen, 1988, Chs. 14-15).

The intriguing and appealing property of taxes on pollution is that, over some range at least, they have negative excess burden: they improve rather than distort the functioning of the market economy. By the proper substitution of environmental taxes for more conventional levies, we can design a more efficent overall system of public revenues. An efficent tax system, therefore, will, in principle, encompass taxes on activities that impose external costs on the environment.

David Terkla (1984), in a study in the United States, has actually developed some measures of the potential efficiency gains from taxes on pollution. Examining a hypothetical set of nationwide taxes on particulate and sulfur oxide emissions from stationary sources in the U.S., Terkla estimates the efficiency gains that would result from using the revenues from these taxes to replace partially those from either the federal income tax (on labor income) or the corporation income tax. He finds that the potential gains from a more efficient overall tax system range from $630 million to over $3 billion in 1982 dollars. These estimates depend, of course, on the specific assumptions concerning the scope and rates of these taxes. A broader set of taxes, including perhaps Green Taxes on carbon emissions, could generate much higher levels of efficiency gains.

The analysis implies that from the expanded perspective of an efficient revenue system, the determination of the optimal level of pollution taxes must take account not only of their role as instruments of environmental management but also their potential for reducing distortions from other taxes. This raises an interesting question. Does this imply that we should set rates on pollution taxes that are higher or lower than the rates that would be set on purely environmental grounds?

Dwight Lee and Walter Misiolek (1986) have provided the answer to this question. We know from the literature on environmental economics that the tax rate, for purely environmental purposes, should be set such that the marginal gains from a cleaner environment equal marginal abatement cost. Lee and Misiolek show that, from the broader optimal tax perspective, this condition must be amended to take account of the reduction in excess burden from other taxes that accompanies the reduced rates on these other sources of revenue. More specifically, the condition for an efficient pollution tax in this expanded framework is that the marginal benefits from a cleaner environment plus the marginal reduction in excess burden on other taxes should equal marginal abatement cost. In short, we must, in setting the levels of pollution taxes, take into account both the value of the improved environmental quality and the gains from a less distorting overall tax system.

This implies that we should generate more revenues from pollution taxes than would be indicated by purely environmental considerations. But what does this imply for the levels of tax rates on polluting activities? As Lee and Misiolek demonstrate, optimal-tax considerations may require either a higher or lower level of pollution tax rates relative to the purely Pigouvian rate that equates marginal environmental gains with marginal abatement costs. The answer depends on tax elasticity. If tax elasticity is greater than unity, then a lower tax rate will generate a higher level of tax revenues--hence, the optimal tax rate on polluting activities will be lower than the purely "environmental rate." Conversely, if tax elasticity falls short of unity, then a higher tax rate will generate more revenues--and the optimal-tax solution will call for a rate higher than the Pigouvian level. For the special case of unitary tax elasticity, the rates will be the same.

Lee and Misiolek turn to the existing empirical literature in environmental economics to see which of these cases is the typical one. The elasticity estimates in this literature do not provide a general answer to the question. The estimates, covering a wide variety of air and water pollutants, exhibit wide variation: some are well below unity, while the upper range for most reaches well above unity. Their interval estimate, for example, of the tax elasticity for the emissions of particualte matter from U.S. electric utilities is 0.99-1.34, suggesting that the rate on this source of emissions would, under an optimal-tax regime, likely be less than the purely environmental charge. It thus appears that there is no general prescription here: an optimal-tax approach is likely, in some instances, to require higher taxes than a purely environmental regime--and, in other cases, lower tax rates. The implication of optimal-tax considerations for the level of environmental quality is unclear.

1.2   Some public choice issues

The optimal-taxation approach to environmental taxation provides a precise theoretical result that involves balancing the gains in environmental quality and reduced excess burden against costs of abatement at the margin. While this result may be unimpeachable in principle, it is somewhat less compelling in a policy setting. To implement the optimal-tax prescription, we would need a very well informed public decision-maker whose interests transcend competing environmental and revenue pressures--an enlightened agent in a position to weigh environmental concerns against revenue needs.

This is a formidable institutional requirement. Environmental management and revenue-raising responsibilities are typically lodged in different agencies within the public sector. In such a setting, it seems unlikely that we will get the systematic weighing of environmental concerns against revenue needs that is envisioned in the optimal-tax theorem. It seems more likely that the responsibility for designing and administering pollution taxes will be lodged either with the environmental authority or with the taxing agency. In the first case, we might expect to see environmental objectives dictate the form and level of the tax, while in the latter case, revenue needs would be more likely to be foremost in the minds of the administering authority.

This suggests some potential for a public-choice approach to this issue. Suppose, for example, that the design and management of pollution taxes were the responsibility of the public revenue authority--the Treasury or a Legislative Tax Committee. To take an extreme case, Brennan and Buchanan (1980) have suggested that we might expect such an agency to behave as a revenue maximizer, a Leviathan seeking to extract the maximum level of revenues. What would such revenue-maximizing behavior imply for the level of tax rates on pollution? The answer (much like earlier) is unclear: it depends on the elasticity of the tax base. If tax elasticity exceeds unity, then a revenue-maximizer will lower the tax rate; if, in contrast, the tax base is inelastic, revenues will be increased by raising the rate.[3] Leviathan, in short, could prove to be either a friend or foe of the environment!

Revenue maximization is admittedly an extreme assumption. We might expect that even a revenue authority would give some consideration to environmental concerns--in response perhaps to the lobbying efforts of concerned groups. It is interesting in this regard that the recent adoption of "eco-taxes" in Sweden took place in an explicitly revenue-neutral setting: existing taxes were, in fact, reduced with the introduction of pollution charges (Barde, 1991, p. 7). Likewise, attempts (although not successful) to introduce environmental taxes in Austria involved the packaging of the proposed levies with proposed cuts in other taxes. In the United States, there is the potential for such coordination in the U.S. Congress where "interested" committees sometimes have joint jurisdiction over certain regulatory programs; the interaction between the Congress and the President on most tax matters provides a further opportunity for an integration of environmental and tax objectives.[4] While such coordination may occur, there remains a potential policy problem here. Pollution taxes, in an optimal-tax framework, serve two ends: an environmental objective and a revenue-raising objective. And it seems quite possible that, in the policy arena, one or the other of them will get the upper hand in the design and management of this policy instrument. I shall return to this issue in the concluding section.

1.3   The linkage issue

The discussion to this point has run in terms of environmental taxes that are designed and attached explicitly to polluting activities. The environmental economics literature is quite specific about the nature of such taxes: they must be per-unit levies applied directly to the waste emissions or other vehicles of environmental damage. Such taxes must be directly <u>linked</u> to the source of the pollution.

In some cases, such a direct linkage may be a relatively easy matter. However, in other circumstances, it may be both difficult and costly to measure and monitor waste emissions. In such cases, the best we can do may involve taxing an input or other activity that is associated with the polluting activity. Such indirect linkages are admittedly not fully satisfactory. A tax, for example, on the sulfur content of coal purchased provides an incentive to use higher grade coal, but it does not encourage the use of scrubbers to treat the emissions as they pass through enter the stack. The tax should, in principle, be attached directly to the emissions that enter the atmosphere.

There is a second reason why such linkages may be indirect. Some taxes may have been enacted for other than environmental purposes. Taxes on gasoline, for example, were originally intended in the U.S. as a source of funds for the construction of highways and other roads. Yet such taxes may well have unintended side effects on the environment. Thus, indirect linkages may come into being unintentionally.

This is an important issue, for, as the next section makes clear, most of the taxes in the United States that have an impact on environmental quality are of the latter variety: their linkage to the environment is indirect in character. This means that in assessing their role as instruments in environmental policy, we must look carefully at the channels through which they impact on the environment and the likely magnitude of their effect.

112

Chapter 2

EXISTING TAXES AND THE ENVIRONMENT

Simply describing the structure of "environmentally relevant" taxes in the United States is not an easy task. The U.S. has a federal system of government with a central government, 50 states, and many thousands of local governments (including counties, cities, municipalities, townships, and special districts). Moreover, the fiscal system in the U.S. is a relatively decentralized one in which lower levels of government play an important role both in the raising and disbursement of revenues. And there is a bewildering variety of tax structures: each state has its own fiscal system with its distinctive forms and mix of taxes. Even where they rely on the same general forms of taxation, state and local governments introduce their specific provisions and rate structures. This makes it difficult (and sometimes misleading) to try to summarize the fiscal structure of the nation in terms of a simple set of summary numbers.

All this variety in fiscal structure, while perhaps somewhat confusing, has an interesting and potentially valuable dimension. The U.S. federal system has been characterized as a "laboratory" in which a multiplicity of experiments are going on at any moment in time. From the results of these various experiments, we may be in a position to learn something about what works and what doesn't work, lessons that may then drawn upon by the other members of the union. With this in mind, I turn to the existing tax structure in the U.S. as it relates to environmental concerns.

2.1   The excise tax on ozone-depleting chemicals

At the central government level, there is one tax that has been designed and introduced for ostensibly environmental reasons (although, as I will suggest, there is some ambiguity here). This is the ozone-depleting chemical tax introduced in conjunction with the Montreal Protocol to phase out emissions of chlorofluorocarbons (CFCs) and halons into the atmosphere. The Montreal Protocol established a schedule under which emissions of these ozone-depleting chemicals will systematically be phased out over the coming decade. More specifically, under the amended Protocol, all but one of these chemicals will be phased out by the year 2,000; the remaining chemical, methyl chloroform, will go out of use by the year 2005. In 1990, the U.S. accelerated this schedule somewhat as part of the Amendments to the Clean Air Act. And, more recently in 1992, President Bush announced that the U.S. will further accelerate the phaseout of ozone-depleting substances well ahead of earlier timetables; the President has urged other countries to join the U.S. in this effort.

The ozone-depleting chemical tax, introduced on January 1, 1990, and extended effective January 1, 1991, is an excise tax imposed on each pound of ozone-depleting chemicals. The exact tax for a specific chemical is determined by taking a <u>base amount</u> for the tax and multiplying it by an <u>ozone-depleting factor</u> applicable to the particular chemical. The base amount rises over time with an initial value of $1.37 per pound in 1990, increasing to $3.10 in 1995 and an additional $0.45 per year thereafter. The chemical-specific multiplication factors range from 0.1 to 10.0 so that the taxes applicable to particular chemicals vary widely in accordance with their presumed contribution to ozone depletion. A complete schedule of these base amounts and ozone-depleting factors appears in Appendix A. The tax is projected to produce revenues of $890 million in 1991, rising to $1,380 million by 1996.

The tax has thus been designed properly from the standpoint of applying a uniform penalty per unit of ozone-depleting potential across all chemicals and uses. But what is interesting, and in a way puzzling, about the tax is that it has been applied on top of a set of quantitative restrictions for the phase-out of these chemicals. From the persepctive of regulating emissions, this will create a redundancy: one of the policy instruments, either the quantity restriction or the tax, will be binding and the other will not. If, for example, the quantity restriction is the binding constraint, then the tax will have no effect on levels of emissions. It will serve solely to raise revenues. This will, incidentally, serve an equity objective: it can capture some of the excess profits that accrue to those in control of the limited supplies of these chemicals. And this is one of the objectives of the tax.

There is apparently some evidence to suggest that the tax may be binding on some uses of these chemicals. One report (OECD 1991) notes that the tax seems to have reduced substantially the demand for CFCs in the manufacture of soft foams and is likely to reduce the use of CFCs in "rigid foam insulation" when the partial exemption for chemicals used in their manufacture expires in 1994. The demand for certain uses of halons, in contrast, appears quite price inelastic because of the absence of good substitutes, and is hence unlikely to be affected by the tax.

2.2   Taxes on gasoline

Gasoline taxes are levied in the United States both by the federal and by state governments, although, even in combination, the total level of tax rates is low by most European standards. The federal tax is currently $.14 per gallon ($.20 per gallon for diesel fuel), while, as Table 2.1 indicates, as of December 1990, state gasoline taxes ranged from a high of $.22 in the states of Connecticut and Washington to a low of $.04 in Florida. The median state tax rate was $.16, suggesting a "typical" federal plus state tax rate of about $.30 per gallon.[5]

Several states have introduced incremental increases in their rates over the last year: fifteen states increased motor fuel or motor vehicle taxes and only one lowered them for fiscal year 1992. These taxes produce sizeable revenues. In fiscal year 1989, the federal excise tax on gasoline and gasohol generated $9.96 billion, while state government revenues from this source were $18.0 billion.

The tax on gasoline was one of the first widely used taxes on commodities by the states in this country (the other is the tax on tobacco products). Oregon first introduced the tax in 1919, and by 1929 it was used by every state in the union. During the 1930s and 1940s, it became the most important single source of tax revenues for state governments, producing over one-quarter of state tax revenues. The federal government introduced a gasoline tax in 1932 (despite vigorous protests from the states) and later expanded the tax as part of the new Highway Trust Fund in 1956.

The primary objective of gasoline taxes has historically not been an environmental one. These taxes have in large part been seen as an equitable way for financing the construction and maintenance of roads and highways; from this perspective, they are sometimes viewed as "user taxes," although taxes paid by a particular driver are surely far from a perfect measure of benefits received.[6] Most of the revenues from these taxes are, in fact, earmarked for transportation programs. The federal government has used the great bulk of the revenues from the Highway Trust Fund for grants-in-aid to state and local governments for the construction of a national system of interstate highways. About 98 percent of the actual spending on highway facilities and services is done by state and local governments.

While the tax is not primarily an instrument for environmental management, it clearly has some side effects on environmental, especially air, quality. As we learned in the 1970s, the price elasticity of demand for gasoline is certainly not zero. With gasoline prices in the United States running at somewhat above $1 per gallon, excise taxes are probably raising the "typical" price of motor fuels in the U.S. by around 25 percent. This has some discernible impact in terms of encouraging the use of more fuel-efficient cars, reducing commuting distances, and increasing the use of mass-transit forms of transportation.

Such changes in behavior reduce auto emissions and contribute to some extent to improved air quality, especially in urban areas. If we take -0.7 as a representative estimate of the long run price elasticity of the demand for gasoline, this suggests that gasoline taxes in the U.S. reduce auto emissions by something on the order of 15 percent. While this is not a huge fraction, it is nevertheless of real importance, since auto emissions are such a major source of urban air pollution. The U.S. could clearly go much farther in this direction (as many OECD countries have done), but there doesn't appear to be much political impetus, at this juncture at least, for such moves (with one exception to be mentioned later).

2.3   Other taxes and charges related to motor vehicle use

In addition to excise taxes on gasoline, federal, state, and local governments impose a variety of other taxes and fees that are related to motor vehicle usage. The federal government levies a 12 percent manufacturers excise tax on trucks and trailers, an annual use tax on "heavy vehicles" (trucks), and an excise tax on tires that weigh in excess of 40 pounds. In addition, there is a federal government "Gas Guzzler" tax on automobiles with unsatisfactory fuel economy ratings. State and local governments (primarily the former) levy a variety of auto taxes and fees. The major items here include annual registration fees for automobiles (ranging from $8 in Arizona and Georgia to $52 in New Jersey), operator's license fees, auto inspection fees, and sales taxes on the purchaes of automobiles.[7] State motor vehicle and license fees raised revenues of $10.15 billion in 1989.

Table 2.1
State Gasoline Taxes: Rates per Gallon, Selected Years, 1978-1991

Region and State	1991	1990	1989	1988	1987	1986	1985	1984	1982	1980	1978
Exhibit: Federal Tax	$.14	$.09	$.09	$.09	$.09	$.09	$.09	$.09	$.04	$.04	$.04
Median	0.18	.16	.16	.145	.145	.13	.12	.12	.10	.09	.08
Alabama+°	0.11	.11	.11	.11	.11	.11	.11	.11	.11	.07	.07
Alaska+°	0.08	.08	.08	.08	.08	.08	.08	.08	.08	.08	.08
Arizona	0.18	.18	.17	.16	.16	.16	.13	.13	.10	.08	.08
Arkansas	0.185	.135	.135	.135	.135	.135	.135	.095	.095	.095	.085
California+o°	0.15	.14	.09	.09	.09	.09	.09	.09	.07	.07	.07
Colorado	0.22	.20	.20	.18	.18	.18	.12	.13	.09	.07	.07
Connecticut°	0.25	.22	.20	.20	.19	.17	.16	.15	.11	.11	.11
Delaware°	0.19	.16	.16	.16	.16	.11	.11	.11	.11	.09	.11
District of Columbia	0.18	.18	.18	.155	.155	.155	.155	.155	.14	.10	.10
Florida+°	0.04	.04	.04	.04	.04	.04	.04	.04	.08	.08	.08
Georgia o°	0.075	.075	.075	.075	.075	.075	.075	.075	.075	.075	.075[a]
Hawaii+o°	0.16	.11	.11	.11	.11	.11	.11	.085	.085	.085	.085
Idaho°	0.22	.19	.18	.18	.145	.145	.145	.145	.125	.095	.095
Illinois+o°	0.19	.13	.13	.13	.13	.13	.13	.12	.075	.075	.075
Indiana o	0.15	.15	.15	.15	.14	.14	.14	.111	.111	.085	.08
Iowa	0.20	.20	.20	.18	.16	.16	.15	.13	.13	.10	.085
Kansas°	0.17	.16	.15	.11	.11	.11	.11	.11	.08	.08	.08
Kentucky°	0.15	.15	.15	.15	.15	.15	.10	.10	.098	.09	.09
Louisiana o	0.20	.20	.20	.16	.16	.16	.16	.16	.08	.08	.08
Maine°	0.19	.17	.17	.16	.14	.14	.14	.14	.09	.09	.09
Maryland	0.185	.185	.185	.185	.185	.135	.135	.135	.11	.09	.09
Massachusetts°	0.21	.17	.11	.11	.11	.11	.11	.11	.104	.085	.085
Michigan	0.15	.15	.15	.15	.15	.15	.15	.15	.11	.11	.09
Minnesota	0.20	.20	.20	.20	.17	.17	.17	.17	.13	.11	.09
Mississippi+°	0.18	.18	.18	.17	.15	.09	.09	.09	.09	.09	.09
Missouri	0.11	.11	.11	.11	.11	.07	.07	.07	.07	.07	.07
Montana+	0.205	.20	.20	.20	.20	.15	.15	.15	.09	.09	.03
Nebraska°	0.234	.214	.22	.182	.176	.19	.164	.149	.137	.105	.095
Nevada+°	0.18	.1625	.1625	.1625	.1425	.1125	.1125	.1025	.1025	.06	.06
New Hampshire	0.18	.16	.14	.14	.14	.14	.14	.14	.14	.11	.10
New Jersey°	0.105	.105	.105	.105	.08	.08	.08	.08	.08	.08	.08
New Mexico+	0.162	.162	.162	.142	.14	.11	.11	.11	.10	.08	.07
New York+o°	0.08	.08	.08	.08	.08	.08	.08	.08	.08	.08	.08
North Carolina°	0.226	.215	.209	.14	.155	.12	.12	.12	.12	.09	.09
North Dakota	0.17	.17	.17	.17	.17	.13	.13	.13	.08	.08	.08
Ohio°	0.21	.20	.18	.148	.147	.12	.12	.12	.117	.07	.07
Oklahoma°	0.16	.16	.17	.16	.16	.10	.10	.09	.0658	.0658	.0658
Oregon+°	0.20	.18	.16	.14	.12	.11	.10	.09	.08	.07	.07
Pennsylvania	0.12	.12	.12	.12	.12	.12	.12	.12	.11	.11	.09
Rhode Island°	0.26	.20	.20	.15	.15	.13	.13	.13	.10	.10	.10
South Carolina	0.16	.16	.16	.15	.15	.13	.13	.13	.13	.10	.09
South Dakota+	0.18	.18	.18	.18	.18	.13	.13	.13	.13	.12	.08
Tennessee+°	0.20	.21	.21	.17	.17	.17	.12	.09	.09	.07	.07
Texas	0.20	.15	.15	.15	.15	.10	.10	.05	.05	.05	.05
Utah°	0.19	.19	.19	.19	.19	.14	.14	.14	.11	.09	.09
Vermont o	0.15	.15	.15	.13	.13	.13	.13	.13	.11	.09	.09
Virginia+o°	0.175	.175	.175	.175	.175	.15	.11	.11	.11	.11	.09
Washington+o°	0.23	.22	.18	.18	.18	.18	.18	.18	.12	.12	.11
West Virginia	0.155	.155	.155	.105	.105	.105	.105	.105	.105	.105	.105
Wisconsin°	0.222	.215	.208	.209	.20	.175	.165	.16	.13	.09	.07
Wyoming	0.09	.09	.09	.08	.08	.08	.08	.08	.08	.08	.08

Note: For 1978-1987, rates are as of July 1; for 1988, October 1; for 1989-1991, December 1.

+ Local taxes may be additional.

o State sales taxes are additional.

Source: Advisory Commission on Intergovernmental Relations, Significant Features of
Fiscal Federalism, 1992 Edition, Vol. I (Washington, D.C.: ACIR, 1992), Table 34,
p. 102

Various states have introduced other vehicle- (or fuel-) related taxes (State Tax Notes, Nov. 11, 1991). Arkansas, for example, recently imposed fees on tires and batteries; likewise, Tennessee has, in fiscal year 1992, imposed a tax on new tire sales. Texas has, this year, introduced a coastal protection fee of 2 cents per barrel on crude oil. There is not available, at this juncture, a systematic inventory of such taxes or fees (more on this later), but many such charges exist (and are being introduced) at state and local levels.

2.4   Severance taxes

Severance taxes are excise taxes levied on the extraction of mineral resources (notably petroleum). These taxes are employed primarily at the state level in the United States. Although 38 states levy severance taxes, they are not a major source of revenue for the states as a whole, accounting for only between 1 and 2 percent of total state general revenues. They are, however, a significant revenue source for a few states, notably Alaska, Louisiana, Texas, and Wyoming. Meiszkowski and Toder (1983) estimate that in 1981 the seven major energy producing states collected about $500 per capita, a sizeable sum, in natural resource revenues. Both the level of rates and the definition of the tax base vary widely among the states.

Severance taxes can affect the environment through the impact that they have on the rates and timing of extraction of mineral resources. Economic theory suggests that these taxes will have two kinds of effects (Deacon, 1990). First, they will discourage both exploration and extraction activities at the margin. The issue here is simply that taxation will render unprofitable those exploration and extraction operations that were barely profitable in the absence of the tax. This effect is called "high-grading" to indicate that "lower-grade" deposits will, under taxation, be ignored. Second, severance taxes alter the time profile of the profit-maximizing pattern of extraction: they "tilt" it toward the future. Relative to the untaxed path, such taxes reduce drilling and output in all periods, but to a greater extent in early, than in more distant, periods. In addition, drilling activity ceases prematurely.

How large are these effects in the United States? Robert Deacon (1990) has undertaken an interesting and suggestive simulation study of the petroleum industry in the U.S. in an attempt to answer this question. The issue is somewhat more complicated because exhaustible resources in this country are subject to three forms of taxation: corporation income taxes, severance taxes, and local property taxes. Deacon finds that corporation income taxes have little effect on extraction rates. In contrast, local property taxes have a real impact. Like severance taxes, they discourage exploration and extraction, but (unlike severance taxes) they encourage earlier extraction. Since under property taxation, the value of the minerals under ground is subject to tax, it pays to get them out of the ground earlier. Deacon's simulations suggest that, overall, the effects of this set of taxes in the U.S. is to reduce levels of exploration and extraction and to tilt the time profile to some extent toward the future. The estimated reduction in total oil production resulting from these taxes is 10 to 15 percent.

It is difficult to translate these findings into a set of clear effects on the environment. About all that can be said is that the lower levels of exploration, development, and extraction activities occasioned by these taxes should result in somewhat less environmental disruption. To say more than this would require a careful study.

2.5   User fees for local solid waste disposal services[8]

There is growing concern in the United States with the problem of disposal of municipal solid wastes. Not only have the quantities of such wastes risen dramatically, but the costs of their disposal have also increased as the capacity of existing landfills has been exhausted, as stricter environmental regulations governing landfills and incinerators have been introduced, and as public aversion to disposal sites has grown. In most communities in the U.S., residential waste services are financed through general revenues (typically through local property taxation) or by flat fees such that the marginal cost of additional refuse to the household is zero.

There is now some interest in, and a limited use of, fees for municipal waste services that vary with the level of refuse discarded. Such fees will, in principle, provide a direct incentive to reduce the household's quantity of solid wastes. A limited number of communities in the U.S. have been experimenting with such fee systems. These systems typically take one of two forms. The first requires households to specify a number of waste containers of a given size per week. Households are then charged for their subscribed number of containers irrespective of how full or heavy the containers are. The second form of these systems requires that all waste containers for pickup be specially marked plastic bags or self-provided containers marked with a sticker or tag. Under this variant, the household is charged a price for the bags (or the stickers or tags) which reflects collection and disposal costs. Both types of fee systems provide some incentive to the household to reduce its level of refuse. One fear, however, is that such a system also encourages illegal dumping of refuse to avoid the fee.

Marginal cost pricing is quite common for commercial solid wastes, but, as noted, relatively rare for residential wastes. The important issue here is the price responsiveness of quantities of refuse. In one recent study, Robin Jenkins (1991) was able to collect data for a sample of communities experimenting with user-pricing schemes and a set of control communities with general-fund financing of waste disposal services. With these data, Jenkins estimated the price elasticity of demand for waste disposal services separately for residential and commercial sources of refuse. Her findings consist of a statistically significant, but modest, response of quantities of refuse to user prices: the estimated price elasticities are -0.12 for residential demand and -0.29 for commercial demand. These findings thus suggest that user fees for solid waste disposal will generate some response in terms of reduced wastes, although not an enormous one. The response may become somewhat larger over time as households become more accustomed, and adjust, to such pricing regimes.

2.6   State fiscal incentives for solid waste disposal

Closely related to local efforts to charge for residential waste pickups are a number of state measures designed to facilitate waste disposal efforts. These measures take a wide variety of forms including tax incentives for recycling, deposit-refund schemes for beverage containers, and state packaging and materials taxes. I shall try to summarize here the nature and extent of these programs in the U.S.

The first class of programs consists of tax incentives for recycling. According to one recent source (American Legislative Exchange Council, 1991), 23 states had such measures as of January,

118

1991. These incentives include tax credits or deductions for investment in recycling equipment, sales tax exemptions for purchases of recycling machinery, and various loans or grants for related activities.

The second group of programs are the so-called "Bottle Bills," or beverage container deposit laws. These measures provide for deposits upon the purchase of beverages that are refundable upon the return of the empty containers. Although such measures have a long history in the U.S., they were "re-introduced" by the State of Oregon in October, 1972. There are now nine states that have such deposit-refund laws. There has been considerable interest in national legislation to provide a nationwide beverage container deposit law. But there exists substantial opposition to such a measure. A recent General Accounting Office report (U.S. GAO, 1990) has examined the "Trade-offs in Beverage Container Deposit Legislation."

The benefits from such deposit programs are largely environmental in character: they reduce litter, conserve energy and natural resources, and reduce the quantites of solid waste going into landfills. Studies of these programs indicate that they have reduced the volume of beverage container litter between 79 and 83 percent and the overall amount of solid waste by as much as 6 percent by weight and up to 8 percent by volume. However, the programs also entail costs. These include additional capital and operating costs to the beverage industry. In addition, there is some concern that deposit programs divert potential revenues away from curbside recycling programs, making the latter economically infeasible.

There have been several studies of the costs and benefits of container deposit legislation, but the studies produce conflicting results on the relative magnitude of benefits and costs. Interestingly, there seems to be widespread national support among the populace for a national beverage container deposit law. The GAO conducted a telephone survey which (along with other surveys) found that the vast majority of Americans would support such legislation. Moreover, the GAO study found that most states with deposit laws also had local curbside recycling programs, suggesting that such deposit measures and curbside recycling can coexist.

Nevertheless, it is hard, on purely economic grounds, to make an airtight case for deposit laws. The GAO concludes that "Although nine states currently have deposit laws and various studies on the effects of these laws have been conducted, we do not believe that the effects of deposit legislation have been quantified to the extent that it can be conclusively determined whether a mandatory national deposit system would be advantageous from a strict cost/benefit standpoint...Given this situation, we believe that the desirability of national beverage container deposit legislation is essentially a public policy decision in which value judgments must be made about the trade-offs between costs and environmental benefits and the desirability of federal involvement in solid waste management, an area that has generally been a local responsibility" (p. 5).

Third, eight states have a variety of packaging and materials taxes. These range from taxes on specific items such as newsprint and beverages to more general taxes on manufacturers, wholesalers, distributors, and retailers.

2.7   Other state environmentally related taxes and fees

There are a host of other, quite diverse taxes and fees that are in various ways, directly or indirectly, related to the environment. A number of states, for example, employ environmental permit fees. In most instances, these are flat fees that entitle the permit recipient to engage in a particular activity (e.g., wastewater discharge). Because of their fixed-sum character, they do not vary with the level of the activity and, hence, do not provide an incentive to reduce levels of waste emissions. They serve rather to deter entry into the activity.

There are a few instances, however, where fees are related to the levels of discharges. The State of New Jersey, for example, has introduced a set of fees for discharges into waterways, where the fees are determined by the Department of Environmental Protection and based on the quantity of the contaminants and their relative risk to public health. Likewise, California levies a water waste discharge permit fee based on type and volume of discharged pollutants. Many of the fee programs are designed to provide revenues for funding environmental programs.

2.8   Other federal excise taxes[9]

There are a few additional federal excise taxes that relate to environmental matters. To finance the Superfund program, which provides for cleaning up abandoned toxic waste sites, the Congress established a trust fund with which the EPA can finance public cleanups. The monies for the trust fund come from a variety of sources, among them some federal excise taxes. The major source is a "feedstock tax" on the petroleum and chemical industries. The feedstock tax is a varying, per-unit levy on a wide range of primary inputs to the production of chemical and petroleum derivatives. This tax was never thought of in terms of its incentive effects; rather, it has been viewed solely as a source of funds for Superfund cleanup operations. The feedstock tax has been supplemented by an "environmental tax," consisting of an assessment on every domestic corporation of 0.12 percent of the corporation's minimum taxable income over $2 million.

In addition, there is a federal excise tax on coal sales of $1.10 per ton for underground mines and $0.55 per ton for surface mines, a tax on crude oil of $0.082 per barrel of domestically produced oil and of $0.117 per barrel of imported crude, a tax on the use of harbors and ports, and a set of excise taxes on sport-fishing equipment, bows and arrows, and firearms. The revenues from most of these excise taxes flow into trust funds for the support of programs related to the taxed activity.

Finally, the federal fiscal system provides "tax-subsidies" for certain environmentally related activities. There are depletion allowances that are taken against tax liabilities for oil and gas production, coal and other hard minerals, and for timber. The tax law also allows energy tax credits for solar, geothermal, and ocean thermal properties and a production credit for alternative fuels.

2.9   A concluding note

As this section has indicated, most of the major tax and other fiscal programs with effects on the environment are state and local programs in the United States. In addition, they are a mixed bag: they vary widely in character and from state to state. This makes it difficult in a report like this to pull together in a systematic and comprehensive way an inventory and assessment of these fiscal programs and their incentive effects. As I have learned in the process of writing this report, such an inventory simply does not exist for state and local programs of "environmental taxes and fees." I have, however, worked closely with the Chief Economist of the National Conference of State Legislatures and others concerned with state and local taxation. In view of the wide and growing interest in this topic of environmental taxes, I hope that this report will provide some stimulus to a new effort in the U.S. to provide a comprehensive and systematic collection of information on state and local environmental taxes and fees.

Chapter 3

THE POLICY DEBATE

This section of the paper explores the central issues figuring in the debate over the use of tax instruments for environmental protection. As noted earlier, the atmosphere for this discussion has shifted in important ways in the United States--it is now much more sympathetic to the use of incentive-based measures for environmental management. The first part of this section examines this new "receptiveness" to market-oriented policy instruments and describes some of its manifestations in the U.S. policy arena. I then take up a series of issues that are central to the ongoing policy debate: quantity versus price instruments, international competitiveness, regulatory federalism (i.e., centralized versus decentralized regulatory management), and equity issues.

3.1 The current policy atmosphere

We have come a long way from the days in which economic incentive approaches to environmental regulation were denounced as "licenses to pollute" or summarily dismissed as "impractical." There is widespread interest in, and considerable support for, incentive-based measures as potential alternatives or supplements to the more traditional command-and-control (CAC) policies. This interest has manifested itself both in the Administration, where (as noted earlier) President Bush has explicitly supported the use of market incentives for environmental protection, and in the U.S. Congress where numerous proposals and bills have been introduced for the use of incentive-based policy instruments. As Hahn and Stavins (1991, p. 20) have put it recently, there are "winds of change from Washington."

In the Administration, this support has taken the form, not only of general statements, but of some concrete proposals including the newly enacted system of tradeable permits to address the acid rain problem under the 1990 Amendments to the Clean Air Act. In the EPA itself, Administrator William Reilly has appointed an Economics Incentives Task Force to seek out new ways to implement market-incentive approaches to environmental regulation. There are at the EPA ongoing studies, for example, of the potential use of incentive-based measures for the control of global warming.

This interest is shared in certain quarters in the U.S. Congress and has manifested itself in the passage by both the House and Senate of the new Amendmendments to the Clean Air Act in which both bodies supported the Administration's proposal for a system of tradeable permits to reduce sulfur dioxide emissions. Under this legislation, sulfur dioxide emissions will be cut by 10 million tons (about 50 percent) over the next decade, and this reduction will be allocated among sources through a market in emissions permits.

A more general interest in economic incentive approaches is evident in a bipartisan study, initiated and sponsored in 1988 by U.S. Senators Timothy Wirth of Colorado and John Heinz of Pennsylvania. This study resulted in an imaginative report ("Harnessing Market Forces to Protect Our Environment: Initiatives for the New President," also known as "Project 88") that suggested a broad range of specific incentive-based measures for environmental management (see Stavins, 1988). More recently, bills have been introduced in the Congress for deposit-refund systems for the recycling of batteries and for the use of tradeable permit systems for dealing with municipal waste-treatment problems.

Interestingly, many of these measures have had some support from a formerly hostile source: environmental advocacy groups. Such groups, in the earlier days of the environmental movement, were virtually unanimous in their outspoken opposition to systems that "put the environment up for sale." But many environmentalists have come to understand and appreciate the potential of pricing incentives for protection of the environment. The Environmental Defense Fund, for example, was an active participant in Project 88 and worked closely with White House Staff in the design of the Administration's Clean Air Act proposal. Several other important national organizations, including the National Audubon Society, the Sierra Club, and the National Resources Defense Council, now support at least certain uses of incentive-based policies. Private industry likewise is showing widespread interest in such measures as a way to reduce the costs of pollution control (Hahn and Stavins, 1991, pp. 25-6).

The sources of this new receptivity to economic incentives are, in part, associated with the "market-oriented" era on which we have entered. With the collapse of many centrally planned economies and their embracing of market principles, there is a widespread sense of the potential efficacy of market approaches to dealing with a wide class of social problems. Incentive-based strategies are in vogue.

Moreover, the more traditional CAC policies have not, in the view of many, been highly successful in resolving our environmental problems. Especially as we attempt to introduce yet more stringent controls in a setting of rising marginal control costs, there is a real concern with finding more efficient ways of achieving our environmental objectives. And economic incentive approaches offer just such a promise. At any rate, the setting is a much more sympathetic one. Nevertheless, many observors still harbor serious reservations. And the policy arena is the site of the debate of many difficult issues concerning the design and implementation of these policy measures. We turn now to some of these issues.

3.2 Quantity versus price instruments

While the general atmosphere in the policy arena has become much more receptive to the use of market-based incentives for environmental protection, the specific form of these instruments has itself been the subject of some interesting and intense debate. As noted earlier, the tendency in the United States has been to opt for the use of so-called quantity instruments (systems of tradeable emissions permits) rather price instruments (fees or taxes).

The rationale for this preference among incentive-based policy instruments is of some interest. Although, in principle, we can achieve the requisite reductions in polluting activities with either systems of tradeable permits or effluent taxes, these two approaches have some important differences in a policy setting. First, the quantity approach gives the environmental authority direct control over the levels of waste discharges. Under the tax approach, the regulator must determine the level of the tax, and if, for example, the tax turns out to be too low, then emissions will exceed the targeted levels. Since environmental objectives or standards are often stated in quantity terms, an agency will find itself in a better position to achieve its regulatory objectives if it has direct control over the quantities of waste emissions rather than indirect control through a price instrument.

This consideration assumes even more significance in an intertemporal setting. In a world of growth and inflation, a specific nominal tax that restricts emissions adequately at one time will fail to do so later in the presence of economic growth and rising prices. The environmental authority will have to enact periodic (and unpopular) increases in tax rates. In contrast, a system of tradeable permits automatically accomodates itself to growth and inflation. Since there is no change in the aggregate supply of emissions permits without explicit action by the environmental regulator, the increased demand for waste emissions will simply translate itself into a higher market-clearing price for permits with no effect on the overall level of discharges.

A second issue has probably been of even greater importance in the United States. New taxes of any sort have been fiercely opposed in the U.S. The proposal (mentioned earlier) for a nationwide system of taxes on sulfur and nitrogen dioxide emissions in 1987 induced an immediate and hostile response from industry (especially public power utilities) and representatives of labor, who made much over the cost increases and lost jobs that they claimed would result from the new taxes. This opposition ultimately doomed the bill. A system of tradeable permits, in contrast, can avoid this source of opposition. If the permits are auctioned off to sources, then, of course, they result in new costs to polluters--just like taxes. But rather than allocating the permits by auction, the environmental authority can choose to distribute these permits freely among existing sources. Some form of "grandfathering" can be used to allocate the permits based on historical performance. Existing firms thus receive a marketable asset, which they can then use either to validate their own emissions or sell to another polluter. Sources are naturally much more receptive to a system that provides them with a valuable asset than to one that imposes a new cost on them. This kind of distribution of permits has, in fact, been employed in the quantity approach in the United States.

And, third, permits have the importance advantage of familiarity. Environmental regulators have had long experience with permits--and it is a much less radical step to make such permits effectively tradeable than to replace the whole system with a set of taxes for environmental management (with which there is virtually no experience). For these three reasons, policy makers in the U.S. have, to this juncture, preferred to adopt quantity rather than price instruments for environmental regulation. There is some reason to believe that taxes are becoming a somewhat more appealing alternative in the current setting--and I will return to this issue in the concluding section of the paper.

3.3   International competitiveness

The issue of international competitiveness has come to the fore in the U.S. in the debate over environmental policy. In particular, the charge is that environmental measures in the United States have burdened domestic industries with additional costs and put them at a competitive disadvantage relative to their counterparts in certain other countries that have a more relaxed environmental posture. Especially in the current period of recession with unemployment running at high rates, U.S. policy makers have become very sensitive to this issue. It has reached the point where actual legislation has been introduced in the U.S. Congress. On April 25, 1991, Senator David Boren of Oklahoma introduced a bill entitled "The International Pollution Deterrence Act of 1991." This bill calls for "countervailing duties" (tariffs) on goods coming into the United States from countries with environmental standards that are less strict than those in the U.S. The amount of the tariff would be equal to the per-unit difference in environmental compliance costs. In introducing the bill, Senator Boren stated that "We are upholding our responsibilities to the world environment but many of our trading partners are not...This means fewer jobs in America as cheaper foreign goods compete with our products and it means more environmental problems for everybody because pollution knows no national boundaries."

These international issues, interestingly, have been the subject of some attention in the environmental economics literature.[10] It is clear, for example, that the introduction of costly abatement measures in <u>some</u> countries can alter the international structure of relative costs with potential effects on patterns of specialization and world trade (e.g., Baumol and Oates, 1988, ch. 16). This general point has taken a more specific form. The concern has become that the less developed countries, with their efforts directed toward economic development rather than environmental protection, will tend to develop a comparative advantage in pollution-intensive industries. The world's dirty industries, according to this view, will find it less costly to locate in the developing countries than in the industrialized nations where they are subject to substantial pollution-control costs. In consequence, the fear is that the developing countries will become "havens" for the world's heavy polluters: this contention is the so-called "pollution-haven hypothesis."

Some early studies, using simulation techniques, tried to estimate the extent of this effect. But we are now in a position to examine what has happened historically, at least to this juncture. Two recent studies, quite different in character, have addressed this issue directly. Jeffrey Leonard (1988), in what is largely a case study of international trade and investment flows for several key industries and countries, finds little evidence that pollution-control measures have exerted a systematic effect on international trade and investment. After examining some aggregate figures, the policy stances in several industrialized and developing countries, and the operations of multinational corporations, Leonard concludes that "the differentials in the costs of complying with environmental regulations and in the levels of environmental concern in industrialized and industrializing countries have not been strong enough to offset larger political and economic forces in shaping aggregate international comparative advantage" (p. 231).

James Tobey (1989, 1990) has studied the same issue in a large econometric study of international trade patterns in "pollution-intensive" goods. After controlling for the effects of relative factor abundance and other trade determinants, Tobey cannot find any effects of the various measures he uses of the stringency of domestic environmental policies. Tobey estimates two sets of equations that explain, respectively, patterns of trade in pollution-intensive goods and <u>changes</u> in trade patterns from 1970 to 1984. In neither set of equations do the variables measuring the stringency of domestic environmental policy have the predicted effect on trade patterns.

Why have domestic environmental measures not induced "industrial flight" and the development of "pollution havens"? The primary reason seems to be that the costs of pollution control have not, in fact, loomed very large, even in heavily polluting industries. Existing estimates

126

suggest that control costs in the U.S. have run on the order of only 1 to 2-1/2 percent of total costs in most pollution-intensive industries; H. David Robison (1985, p. 704), for example, reports that total abatement costs per dollar of output in the United States were well under 3 percent in all industries with the sole exception of electric utilities where they were 5.4 percent. Such small increments to costs are likely to be swamped in their impact on international trade by the much larger effects of changing differentials in labor costs, swings in exchange rates, etc. Moreover, nearly all the industrialized nations have introduced environmental measures--and at roughly the same time--so that such measures have not been the source of significant cost differentials among major competitors. There seems not to have been a discernible movement in investment in these industries to the developing countries because major political and economic uncertainties have apparently loomed much larger in location decisions than have the modest savings from less stringent environmental controls.

In short, domestic environmental policies, <u>at least to this point in time</u>, do not appear to have had significant effects on patterns of international trade. This is a comforting finding in one respect. It suggests that too much is being made of this issue in the policy arena. Especially in difficult economic times, it is easy to see why politicians may find such issues an attractive way to deflect concern and blame away from more fundamental domestic ills. But the evidence does not appear to support their claims.

3.4   Regulatory federalism

In the context of a federal system of government with a substantial degree of fiscal and regulatory decentralization, there is considerable concern and interest in the United States in the respective roles of federal, state, and local government in environmental management. For issues that clearly transcend local and state boundaries (such as acid-rain problems), a major role for centralized management is clearly in order. But many environmental problems are of a local character: the emissions of certain air and water pollutants, for example, result in environmental damages that are limited mainly to the area at or around the site of their discharge. For such forms of pollution, there is a real case for decentralized environmental regulation.

This issue has manifested itself in terms of an intriguing anomoly in U.S. environmental legislation. Under the Clean Air Act in 1970, the U.S. Congress instructed the Environmental Protection Agency to set uniform national standards for air quality: maximum permissible concentrations of key air pollutants applicable to all areas in the nation. But two years later under the Clean Water Act, the Congress decided to let the individual states determine their own standards (subject to EPA approval) for water quality. This poses the important question of the locus of regulatory authority: Should environmental decision-making be centralized or left to state and local government?

Basic economic principles appear to suggest a straightforward answer to the question. For those environmental phenomena which are essentially localized in terms of their effects, the optimal standards for environmental quality are likely to vary among jurisdictions in accordance with local preferences and cost conditions. An optimal outcome will thus involve differentiated environmental standards across jurisdictions that reflect these basic cost and taste differences. From this perspective, uniform national standards cannot achieve an optimal outcome. What is needed is a system of "regulatory federalism" that places the responsibility and authority for environmental management at the appropriate level for each form of polluting activity.

Some environmental economists, such as John Cumberland (1981), have objected to this general proposition on the grounds of political naivete. Their claim is that in their eagerness to attract new business investment and jobs, state or local officials will tend to set excessively lax environmental standards: they will set tax rates on polluting levels of activities that are too low or quantities of tradeable permits that are too high. The fear, in short, is that economic competition among states and localities will undermine efforts for environmental protection.

This issue has been the subject of some recent attention in the environmental economics literature.[11] Oates and Schwab (1988a, 1988b), for example, have constructed a series of prototypical models of economic competition among decentralized jurisdictions that involve both fiscal and environmental policy variables. The basic outcomes in these models do not exhibit the kinds of distortions that Cumberland and others fear: decision-makers in these models choose standards for environmental quality for which marginal benefits equal marginal cost. However, these results are not especially robust: it is easy to introduce plausible modifications that can result in excessive environmental degradation.

At the policy level, there is continuing concern with this issue. State and local governments continue to play a major role in the management of U.S. environmental programs, but there is a real tension in the balance between centralized and decentralized authority. To cite one case, it has become increasingly clear that the costs of requiring Southern California to meet the same standards for air quality as the rest of the nation are exhorbitant and unreasonable. The geography and economy there combine in ways to make clean air far more expensive than elsewhere. But, instead of recognizing the special circumstances of the Southern California basin, U.S. officials have responded by extending the time schedule for compliance, and Southern California continues adopting new measures, unjustifiable on any sort of benefit-cost calculation, and with no prospect of ever attaining the national standards. The cost, in such cases, of ignoring the need for environmental federalism is likely to be very high.

3.5 Equity issues

In the debate over the the 1987 House Bill for a national tax on sulfur and nitrogen oxide emissions, the opposition raised as one objection to the tax its potential regressivity. They contended that it would substantially drive up the utility bills of individual households and that this would fall much more heavily on lower, than on higher, income households. Such arguments are frequently voiced in the debate over new environmental measures, expecially tax measures. And this raises two important questions. Are environmental regulations, and especially taxes on polluting activities, likely to be regressive in their pattern of incidence? In short, is this claim true? And, second, if it is true, what sorts of alternatives, if any, are available to soften the adverse redistributive impact of these policies?

The redistributive implications of environmental programs can raise some very complicated and tricky issues.[12] But there is some evidence to suggest that the costs of the major existing programs for the control of air and water pollution in the United States have, in fact, had a regressive

128

pattern of incidence. To take one careful study, H. David Robison (1985) examined the distribution of the costs of industrial pollution abatement in a full general-equilibrium framework. Using a highly disaggregated input-output model, Robison assumed that the control costs in each industry were passed forward in the form of higher prices. He was then able to trace these price increases through a general-equilibrium system to determine their effect on the prices of various consumer goods. Robison's model divides individuals into twenty income classes, and, for each class, he had data describing the pattern of consumption in considerable detail. With this information, he was able to estimate for each of his income classes the increase in the prices of the items that they purchase. He finds that the pattern of incidence of control costs is quite regressive. Costs as a fraction of income fall over the whole range of income classes: they range from 0.76 percent of income for his lowest income class to 0.16 percent of income for the highest income classes. Other studies have obtained similar findings, thus giving some substance to the claim that pollution-control measures (including taxes) are likely to be regressive in their incidence.

There are certainly some ways to address the issue of the undesirable distribution of the costs of environmental programs. Some programs have "transitional effects" that hit certain groups much harder than others. Programs, for example, to reduce airborne sulfur emissions may put substantial numbers of coal miners out of work. Such shifting patterns of employment with transitional job losses can be very painful indeed. These transitional costs suggest the need for some form of "adjustment assistance," including unemployment compensation, retraining programs, and perhaps relocation assistance to help those who suffer from altered patterns of output and employment. Such programs are familiar accompanyments to legislation for the reduction of tariffs and other trade restrictions.

More generally, the regressive pattern of price changes (of the sort indicated by the Robison study) will require companion measures if their redistributive impact is to be neutralized. To take an example from the earlier discussion, a proposed system of pollution taxes can be accompanied by cuts in other taxes to make the overall measure revenue neutral. There is an opportunity here to make these cuts in other taxes so as to provide the most generous relief to lower income groups. The pollution taxes might, for example, be packaged with tax credits to low income groups or reductions in the lowest income tax rates.

While such supplementary measures can offset the undesired redistributive impact of pollution taxes, it is critical that such amendments do not compromise the basic incentives provided by the environmental measures themselves. It is important to remember that the basic objectives of taxes on pollution (or other environmental programs) are allocative in nature: their purpose is to achieve important targets for environmental quality. Such measures are often not well suited to achieving redistributional goals. Where their adverse redistributional impact can be easily addressed, it is surely important to do so, but environmental measures should not, in general, be side-tracked on redistributional grounds. We have other policy tools for dealing with the distribution of income.

Chapter 4

TAXES AND THE ENVIRONMENT: AN ASSESSMENT

To conclude this report, I will return to a number of issues in the design and introduction of tax measures that seem to me important if we are to make better use of the tax system for environmental protection. There are, I believe, some real opportunities on the horizon to make some useful steps in this direction. I shall begin with a further exmination of the choice among incentive-based policy instruments and will then proceed to some other important matters in the actual design of environmentally "sensitive" tax policies.

4.1   Quantity versus price instruments again

In the preceding section, I indicated why, it seems to me, regulators in the United States have opted for systems of tradeable permits rather than taxes for environmental management. However, based on this experience and on some further considerations, I think that taxes now stand in a somewhat more favorable light. I see three significant reasons for this. First, the U.S. experience with Emissions Trading has encountered a troublesome obstacle in the actual operation of permit markets. These markets have frequently failed to operate as smoothly as envisioned in theory. In particular, permit markets have often been very thin, especially on the supply side. Robert Hahn (1989) contends that this has been largely the result of unfortunate restrictions on trading that have clouded definitions of property rights and raised serious uncertainties about the ability to obtain these rights in the marketplace when needed. In addition, the number of potential participants in some of these relatively localized markets has often been small with certain large sources in a position to exercise monopolistic influence on permit prices. The thinness of these markets and infrequency of transactions suggests that sources may not observe a clear, well defined price signal to indicate the opportunity costs of their emissions. The absence of such a clear price can impair the effective functioning of the permit system. A regime of effluent taxes, in contrast, encounters no such problems: the tax itself provides a clear, unambiguous measure of the cost of emissions. There is no need to worry about the way the market "works."

A second issue that seems to favor taxes over permits concerns the use of these policy instruments in a setting of uncertainty.[13] Use of a quantity instrument like permits gives the environmental authority a firm control over the aggregate level of polluting emissions. However, in a setting of imperfect information and uncertainty about the costs and benefits of pollution control, the regulator may not have a very good idea about the costs that such a quantity approach will impose on sources. In contrast, under tax regime, there is a well defined limit on the costs that will be imposed on sources, for polluters can always elect to pay the tax and not reduce emissions further. The tax constitutes an upper limit to the costs to polluters; there is no such upper limit under a permit system. Conversely, however, the limit on costs under the tax approach introduces uncertainty as to the quantity of emissions, since the regulator is unsure as to the precise way in which sources will respond to the tax. The regulator does not know the exact proportions by which sources will choose to reduce emissions or pay taxes.

The issue here is which form of uncertainty, uncertainty over costs or uncertainty over the level of emissions, is likely to be the more threatening?[14] The answer to this question depends on the particular character of the environmental damages and of the control costs associated with the form of pollution. Suppose, for example, that the nature of the damages is such that important environmental threshold effects exist. If pollutant concentrations exceed some critical value, then an environmental disaster occurs. In such a setting, it is obviously crucial to have careful control over the quantity of waste emissions. The use of environmental taxes could be very dangerous, for if the tax were set too low, emissions could exceed the critical level with catastrophic results. In such instances, it is best to employ a quantity system under which the regulator has direct control over the level of emissions and can avoid the uncertainty over quantity that accompanies the use of a price instrument (such as an effluent charge).

In contrast, in other settings, the damages from additional emissions may be relatively stable over the relevant range; the potential damage from being off a bit on the quantity of emissions will, in such cases, be modest. However, it may be that the marginal costs of pollution control vary dramatically. There exist, in fact, many estimates of the marginal costs of emissions control which indicate that, after a relatively constant range, marginal costs begin to increase sharply. In this setting, the more pressing danger from a mistake in policy is one of excessive costs. If the regulator sets too tough a standard for emissions reductions, he may impose enormous costs on sources. The danger, in this case, is greater with the quantity instrument, for if the supply of permits is set too low, then excessive control costs will be forced upon polluting firms. Under a fee regime, this danger is avoided, since sources can always opt to pay the fee and avoid the more costly controls.

Which of these two dangers is the more prevalent? It is impossible to be completely general on this, but there is, I think, a strong presumption that for many cases of pollution, the larger threat is from excessive costs. Few environmental phenomena seem to be characterized by critical threshold levels over the relevant range of pollution; if we are off by a bit from our environmental targets, the consequences are typically not too serious. In contrast, there is considerable evidence suggesting that existing environmental programs have already induced extensive abatement efforts and that these efforts have pushed us onto the rapidly rising portions of marginal abatement cost curves. Decisions that involve excessively stringent control measures (e.g., too few permits) have the potential to be inordinately costly. And this makes a strong case for a reliance on price, rather than quantity, instruments. In a policy setting characterized by uncertainty, pollution taxes probably provide us with greater protection from serious error than do systems of tradeable permits.

Third, taxes provide public revenues. Although there is strong opposition to new taxes, there is also an almost desperate need for new revenue sources to reduce the budgetary deficit in the United States. Their revenue potential thus gives environmental taxes some real appeal in the current policy setting. For all these reasons, I think that the tax approach is likely to get a more sympathetic hearing in the U.S. than it has in the past. Current policy discussion and analysis is certainly including taxes among the important candidates for incentive-based approaches to environmental protection.

4.2   On the design of environmental tax measures

I introduced in the initial section the issue of the locus of management of environmental taxes. Ideally, in the spirit of the optimal tax approach to this issue, the design and administration of the tax should reflect both environmental and taxation objectives. The tax rate should be set so as realize the joint gains from pollution control and a reduced reliance on distorting taxes. In practice, however, such an integrated approach to tax policy may not always be possible. Where a choice must be made on the locus of the authority for pollution taxation, I think that there are compelling reasons for giving environmental regulators a dominant role in the design and administering of such taxes, rather than assigning responsibility to a taxing agency.

Pollution taxes are a potentially powerful and effective tool for environmental management. There is now a large theoretical and empirical literature that makes a persuasive case for an extensive reliance on economic incentives for pollution control.[15] To remove pollution taxes from the sphere of the environmental authority is effectively to place one of the primary determinants of levels of waste emissions +under the management of another public agency. This is likely to constrain quite severely the policy options for environmental management; it will force environmental regulators to turn to less effective command-and-control instruments for pollution control.

Tax authorities, in contrast, have a substantial range of tax bases from which to choose. Revenues from environmental taxes can ultimately finance only a modest portion of the public budget. This suggests, in my view, that it makes sense for the tax authority to leave tax rates on pollution to the discretion of environmental regulators. The tax authority would view the revenues from such pollution taxes as an exogenous (but welcome) revenue source--and would then determine rates on other tax bases so as to produce the requisite overall level of revenues. I stress here that pollution taxes, effectively employed for purposes of environmental management, can be the source of sizeable revenues. And the "side benefits" in terms of a less distorting tax system can be quite substantial.

Another potentially complex and delicate issue that arises in the design of environmental taxes is the matter of earmarking of funds. As Robert Hahn (1989) and others note, where pollution taxes have been employed in such countries as France, Germany, and the Netherlands for water quality management, the revenue aspect of these taxes has been of central importance. Environmental authorities have typically set tax rates in such a way as to generate the revenues needed for various pollution-control programs. They have looked on these taxes as a source of monies to fund projects for water-quality management, not primarily as instruments for the regulation of waste flows.[16] This earmarking (or creation of "trust funds") for the revenues from environmental taxes is a typical element in legislation for such taxes. In the 1987 U.S. Bill mentioned earlier for a national tax on sulfur and nitrogen oxide emissions, there was a provision to direct the revenues collected from the tax into a special "Sulfur and Nitrogen Emissions Trust Fund" which would be used to assist polluters in meeting their control costs.

Such provisions have a certain appeal in the policy arena. To the extent that the funds are used for financing environmental "cleanup" projects, they are consistent with the OECD "Polluter Pays Principle." Moreover, as Jean-Philippe Barde has suggested to me, such trust funds may serve as a kind of second-best measure where the heavy costs of taxes makes their introduction infeasible without some form of earmarking assistance.

133

At the same time, earmarking has some very troubling aspects. One of the arguments for environmental taxes is the potential improvement in the overall tax system that results from the substitution of revenues from these sources for the funds from other distorting taxes. If the revenues from pollution taxes are siphoned off into increased spending for environmental projects, then they will obviously make no contribution to the enhancement of the overall tax system by reducing the reliance on distorting taxes. The revenues may (as some public-choice writers fear) simply serve to expand the public budget.

Such trust funds may have other perverse allocative effects. In the proposed U.S. bill, a primary use of the revenues would have been to assist polluters in covering their control costs. From the perspective of economic efficiency, this is misplaced assistance. The tax is itself to serve as a signal to polluters to guide their decisions on levels of control activities. Rebates on control costs would distort this signal. Morever, over the longer haul, it is important that polluters bear the full cost of their abatement activities and pollution taxes so that profits (net of costs) will provide the right incentives for entry and exit into the industry (Baumol and Oates, 1988, pp. 52-4).

This is, of course, not to be taken to mean that important environmental projects should not be undertaken. But they should have to meet the same budgetary and economic tests as other public projects. They should not be undertaken simply by virtue of the availability of some earmarked funds.

My own sense then is that, as a rule, earmarking (or the creation of trust funds) should probably be discouraged in the design of environmental taxes. It is better that the revenues be directed into the "general fund" and used as a means to reduce reliance on other distorting forms of taxation.

4.3   Environmental taxes: some specifics

In this part of the paper, I shall suggest a few areas where, it seems to me, that environmental taxation has some potential in the United States. The treatment is neither comprehensive nor in depth; my intent is simply to point to a few uses of environmental taxes that appear promising and that merit further study.

i)   Heavier taxation of gasoline and other fuels. Both the federal and state governments in the U.S. tax gasoline and other fuels for motor vehicles and aircraft, but the taxes rates are low relative to their counterparts in most Europe countries. Although the demand for gasoline appears to be price inelastic, it is far from perfectly inelastic. The price response over the longer haul to higher gasoline prices is substantial and can have a marked impact on the fuel efficiency of vehicles, commuting patterns, and location decisions. In short, such taxes reduce fuel use and thereby reduce air pollution and other congestion and noise problems associated with automobiles. There doesn't appear to be a strong impetus in the U.S. to move in this direction, with the exception, perhaps, of a general carbon tax to be discussed shortly.

ii)   Taxes to increase the fuel efficiency of motor vehicles. There is presently a federal Gas Guzzler excise tax on cars that do not meet specified fuel efficiency standards. There is no tax, however, on cars that meet the standard. A schedule of taxes with rates that decline as fuel efficiency rises could provide a continuing incentive for improving the fuel efficiency of the whole fleet of motor vehicles.

iii) Taxes on various fertilizers and pesticides that result in polluting runoff into rivers, lakes, and bays. The control of various forms of non-point source pollution, notably agricultural runoff, is a serious problem. It is difficult to tax such runoff directly, but a second-best approach involves the taxation of agricultural inputs that have the potential for contributing to such runoff. Such taxes can provide an incentive to seek other forms of farming and pest management.

iv) A wider use of deposit-refund systems to encourage the proper disposal of environmentally damaging wastes. Interesting candidates include lead batteries, tires, and autos themselves (as in Sweden). In addition, the Project 88 report (see Stavins, 1988) recommends such a system for "containerizable hazardous wastes."

v) Waste-end taxes. In addition to (or in place of) "front-end" taxes on inputs into waste generating activities (like the Superfund "feedstock taxes"), there may be a useful place for taxes levied after the generation of wastes at the disposal stage. Such taxes can influence both the level of generation of wastes and disposal practices. A central problem to be addressed here is the incentive that such a tax can create for illegal dumping.

vi) Tax credits for the introduction of less polluting agricultural techniques. Again, because of the difficulty in taxing runoff directly, second-best methods are needed to address the problem. The use of tax credits for investments in agricultural technology that reduce the runoff of pollutants has real potential.

vii) Effluent taxes on discharges of major air and water pollutants. Although the U.S. has opted for systems of tradeable permits for the regulation of certain air and water pollutants, I don't think that we should take this as a closed issue. There remains a case for effluent taxes, and it deserves further study and discussion.

4.4   International issues

It seems suitable to conclude this report with a brief discussion of the international dimensions of U.S. tax policy for the environment. There is a growing concern with global issues that is manifesting itself in a move towards an "open-economy environmental economics" (Oates, 1991). The concern with ozone depletion, leading to the Montreal Protocol, and now the threat of global warming point to the need for international cooperation in addressing the future of the planet.

This has set off a lively policy debate in the United States, as in the rest of the world. Of central interest here, it has led to the study of proposals for a carbon tax, of a national or, perhaps, international scope (Poterba, 1991). For example, the U.S. Congressional Budget Office (1990) has published the results of an extensive study of the taxation of fossil fuels in the U.S. Similar studies are underway in other government agencies, notably the EPA, and also in research institutes and academia. Again, a major issue in the debate is the choice between policy instruments: taxes versus systems of tradeable permits.

Should policy makers opt for the tax approach to regulate carbon emissions, they will acquire a tax base with massive potential for tax revenues. Many of the issues treated in this paper will have to be addressed: Who administers the tax? How is the rate determined? What is to be done with the revenues?

Tax policy over the coming decades has the potential to exert a powerful influence on the course of the environment, both at the national and global levels.

Notes

1. H.R. 2497, the "Sulfur and Nitrogen Emissions Tax Act of 1987," introduced on May 21, 1987.

2. President Bush has expressed his strong opposition to _any_ new taxes at this juncture. But this obviously doesn't rule out new non-tax incentive-based measures, or _perhaps_ some revenue-neutral tax reforms of the sort to be discussed later in the paper.

3. For a more thorough discussion of this case, see Oates (forthcoming).

4. Agency interaction, for example, is evident in the case of Superfund taxes where the EPA has played a major role in the design of the taxes, although they are administered by the Internal Revenue Service.

5. In addition, there are a few states in which local governments also levy excise taxes on gasoline. These taxes are typically at a relatively low rate with the exception of Hawaii where local taxes range from from $.088 to $.165 per gallon.

6. According to the Department of Transportation, in 1985 about 75 percent of the funding for highway expenditures came from highway user taxes and tolls (largely taxes on gasoline), income from invested funds, and proceeds of transportation bond sales. Motor fuel taxes cover a little more than half of total highway expenditures. See Ronald Fisher (1988, ch. 19).

7. In some states, motor vehicles are also subject to state and/or local property taxation. See Appendix B.

8. The material in this section is based on a recent Ph. D. dissertation at the University of Maryland by Robin R. Jenkins (1991).

9. For a useful summary and description of federal environmental tax policy, see U.S. Joint Committee on Taxation (1990).

10. See the survey paper by Cropper and Oates (1992) for a summary of this work.

11. See Cropper and Oates (1992) for a survey of this literature.

12. See Baumol and Oates (1988, ch. 15) for a systematic consideration of these issues.

13. See Martin Weitzman (1974) for the formal genesis of this point.

14. As Weitzman (1974) has shown, the formal answer to this question depends on the relative slopes of the marginal benefit and marginal abatement cost functions. I present the intuition underlying the Weitzman theorem in the text.

15. See Cropper and Oates (1992) for a recent survey of this literature.

16. There are a few instances in which incentive effects have figured importantly in environmental taxes: fees on discharges into Dutch river basins and some of the new "eco taxes" in Sweden on carbon and other airborne emissions. But these appear to be the exception rather than the rule.

Annex 1[1]

The tax per pound of each ozone-depleting chemical is determined by multiplying the <u>base tax amount</u> for the applicable year times the <u>ozone-depleting factor</u> specific to the chemical. The base amounts per pound (in U.S. dollars per pound) rise over time according to the following schedule:

	1990	1991	1992	1993	1994	1995
Chemicals Restricted by the Original Protocol	1.37	1.37	1.67	2.65	2.65	3.10
Chemicals Restricted by the Amended Protocol	-	1.37	1.37	1.67	3.00	3.10

where the base amounts increase by $0.45 per year after calendar 1995.

The ozone-depleting factors are normalized on CFC-11 and are as follows:

Chemicals Restricted by the Original Protocol	Ozone Depleting Factor
CFC-11	1.0
CFC-12	1.0
CFC-113	0.8
CFC-114	1.0
CFC-115	0.6
Halon-1211	3.0
Halon-1301	10.0
Halon-2402	6.0

Chemicals Restricted by the Amended Protocol	Ozone Depleting Factor
CFC-13	1.0
CFC-111	1.0
CFC-112	1.0
CFC-211, 212, 213, 214, 215,	1.0
216, 217	1.0
Carbon Tetrachloride	1.1
Methyl Chloroform	0.1

---

[1] The data and information presented in this appendix and in the text on the excise tax on ozone-depleting chemicals comes from OECD (1991).

The ozone-depleting factor for a particular chemical (for example, 0.8 for CFC-113) is multiplied times the base amount to determine the tax for the chemical in a specific year (e.g., the tax per pound on CFC-113 in 1992 would be 0.8 times 1.67 or 1.336).

A different set of base amounts and ozone-depleting factors has been determined for halons and chemicals used in rigid foam insulation. For the years 1991-93, the tax on these chemicals is approximately $0.25 per pound.

The taxes are projected to generate substantial revenues. The estimates of these revenues by fiscal year:

1991	$ 890 million
1992	1,000 "
1993	1,430 "
1994	1,640 "
1995	1,530 "
1996	1,380 "

Bibliography

American Legislative Exchange Council, *Legislative Update: State Solid Waste Policy: January, 1991*, Washington, D.C., 1991.

BARDE, Jean-Philippe, The Use of Economic Instruments for Environmental Protection in OECD Countries, unpublished paper (1991).

BAUMOL, William J., and Oates, Wallace E., *The Theory of Environmental Policy*, Second Edition (Cambridge: Cambridge University Press, 1988).

BRENNAN, Geoffrey, and Buchanan, James, *The Power to Tax: Analytical Foundations of a Fiscal Constitution* (Cambridge: Cambridge University Press, 1980).

CROPPER, Maureen L., and Oates, Wallace E., "Environmental Economics: A Survey," *Journal of Economic Literature*, 30, June, 1992), pp. 675-740.

CUMBERLAND, John H., "Efficiency and Equity in Interregional Environmental Management," *Review of Regional Studies*, No. 2 (1981), pp. 1-9.

DEACON, Robert T., Taxation, Depletion, and Welfare: A Simulation Study of the U.S. Petroleum Resource, Working Paper No. ENR 90-10, Resources for the Future, Washington, D.C. (June 1990).

FISHER, Ronald C., *State and Local Public Finance* (Glenview, Illinois: Scott, Foresman, and Co., 1988).

HAHN, Robert W. "Economic Prescriptions for Environmental Problems: How the Patient Followed the Doctor's Orders," *Journal of Economic Perspectives*, 3 (Spring, 1989), pp. 95-114.

HAHN, Robert W., and Stavins, Robert N., "Incentive-Based Environmental Regulation: A New Era from an Old Idea?" *Ecology Law Quarterly* 18, No. 1 (1991), pp. 1-42.

JENKINS, Robin R., Municipal Demand for Solid Waste Disposal Services: The Impact of User Fees, Ph.D. Dissertation, University of Maryland (1991).

LEE, Dwight R., and Misiolek, Walter S., "Substituting Pollution Taxation for General Taxation: Some Implications for Efficiency in Pollution Taxation," *Journal of Environmental Economics and Management 13* (Dec., 1986), pp. 338-347.

LEONARD, H. Jeffrey, *Pollution and the Struggle for the World Product* (Cambridge: Cambridge University Press, 1988).

MIESZKOWSKI, Peter, and Toder, E., "Taxation of Energy Resources," in C. McLure and P. Mieszkowski, eds., *Fiscal Federalism and the Taxation of Natural Resources* (Lexington, Mass.: Heath-Lexington, 1983).

OATES, Wallace E., Global Environmental Management: Towards An Open Economy Environmental Economics, University of Maryland, Dept. of Economics Working Paper No. 91-17 (1991).

OATES, Wallace E., "Pollution Charges as a Source of Public Revenues," in H. Giersch, ed., *Economic Evolution and Environmental Concerns* (forthcoming).

OATES, Wallace E., and Schwab, Robert M., Economic Competition Among Jurisdictions: Efficiency Enhancing or Distortion Inducing?" Journal of Public Economics 35 (April 1988a), pp. 333-354.

OATES, Wallace E., and Schwab, Robert M., The Theory of Regulatory Federalism: The Case of Environmental Management, University of Maryland, Dept. of Economics Working Paper No. 88- 26 (1988b).

POTERBA, James M., "Tax Policy to Combat Global Warming: On Designing a Carbon Tax," in R. Dornbusch and J. Poterba, eds., *Global Warming: Economic Policy Responses* (Cambridge, Mass.: M.I.T. Press, 1991), pp. 71-98.

ROBISON, H. David, "Who Pays for Industrial Pollution Abatement?" *Review of Economics and Statistics 67* (Nov., 1985), pp. 702-6.

ROSEN, Harvey S., *Public Finance*, Second Edition (Homewood, Illinois: Irwin, 1988).

State Tax Notes (Nov. 11, 1991) (Arlington, Va.: Tax Analysts).

STAVINS, Robert H., ed., Project 88--Harnessing Market Forces to Protect Our Environment: Initiatives for the New President. A Public Policy Study Sponsored by Senator Timothy E. Wirth, Colorado, and Senator John Heinz, Pennsylvania (Washington, D.C., Dec., 1988).

TERKLA, David, "The Efficiency Value of Effluent Tax Revenues," *Journal of Environmental Economics and Management 11* (June, 1984), pp. 107-23.

TOBEY, James A., The Impact of Domestic Environmental Policies on International Trade, Ph.D. Dissertation, University of Maryland, 1989.

TOBEY, James A., "The Effects of Domestic Environmental Policies on Patterns of World Trade: An Empirical Test," *Kyklos 43* (No. 2), pp. 191-209.

WEITZMAN, Martin L., "Price vs. Quantities," *Review of Economic Studies* 41 (Oct., 1974), pp. 477-91.

U.S. Congressional Budget Office, Carbon Charges as a Response to Global Warming: The Effects of Taxing Fossil Fuels (Washington, D.C.: U.S. GPO, 1990).

U.S. General Accounting Office, <u>Trade-offs in Beverage Container Deposit Legislation</u> (Washington, D.C., Nov. 14, 1990).

U.S. Joint Committee on Taxation, <u>Present Law and Background Relating to Federal Environmental Tax Policy</u> (Washington, D.C.: U.S. Government Printing Office, March 1, 1990).

MAIN SALES OUTLETS OF OECD PUBLICATIONS
PRINCIPAUX POINTS DE VENTE DES PUBLICATIONS DE L'OCDE

ARGENTINA – ARGENTINE
Carlos Hirsch S.R.L.
Galería Güemes, Florida 165, 4° Piso
1333 Buenos Aires   Tel. (1) 331.1787 y 331.2391
Telefax: (1) 331.1787

AUSTRALIA – AUSTRALIE
D.A. Information Services
648 Whitehorse Road, P.O.B 163
Mitcham, Victoria 3132   Tel. (03) 873.4411
Telefax: (03) 873.5679

AUSTRIA – AUTRICHE
Gerold & Co.
Graben 31
Wien I   Tel. (0222) 533.50.14

BELGIUM – BELGIQUE
Jean De Lannoy
Avenue du Roi 202
B-1060 Bruxelles   Tel. (02) 538.51.69/538.08.41
Telefax: (02) 538.08.41

CANADA
Renouf Publishing Company Ltd.
1294 Algoma Road
Ottawa, ON K1B 3W8   Tel. (613) 741.4333
Telefax: (613) 741.5439
Stores:
61 Sparks Street
Ottawa, ON K1P 5R1   Tel. (613) 238.8985
211 Yonge Street
Toronto, ON M5B 1M4   Tel. (416) 363.3171
Telefax: (416)363.59.63
Les Éditions La Liberté Inc.
3020 Chemin Sainte-Foy
Sainte-Foy, PQ G1X 3V6   Tel. (418) 658.3763
Telefax: (418) 658.3763

Federal Publications Inc.
165 University Avenue, Suite 701
Toronto, ON M5H 3B8   Tel. (416) 860.1611
Telefax: (416) 860.1608
Les Publications Fédérales
1185 Université
Montréal, QC H3B 3A7   Tel. (514) 954.1633
Telefax : (514) 954.1635

CHINA – CHINE
China National Publications Import
Export Corporation (CNPIEC)
16 Gongti E. Road, Chaoyang District
P.O. Box 88 or 50
Beijing 100704 PR   Tel. (01) 506.6688
Telefax: (01) 506.3101

DENMARK – DANEMARK
Munksgaard Book and Subscription Service
35, Nørre Søgade, P.O. Box 2148
DK-1016 København K   Tel. (33) 12.85.70
Telefax: (33) 12.93.87

FINLAND – FINLANDE
Akateeminen Kirjakauppa
Keskuskatu 1, P.O. Box 128
00100 Helsinki

Subscription Services/Agence d'abonnements :
P.O. Box 23
00371 Helsinki   Tel. (358 0) 12141
Telefax: (358 0) 121.4450

FRANCE
OECD/OCDE
Mail Orders/Commandes par correspondance:
2, rue André-Pascal
75775 Paris Cedex 16   Tel. (33-1) 45.24.82.00
Telefax: (33-1) 45.24.81.76   or (33-1) 45.24.85.00
Telex: 640048 OCDE

OECD Bookshop/Librairie de l'OCDE :
33, rue Octave-Feuillet
75016 Paris   Tel. (33-1) 45.24.81.67
(33-1) 45.24.81.81
Documentation Française
29, quai Voltaire
75007 Paris   Tel. 40.15.70.00
Gibert Jeune (Droit-Économie)
6, place Saint-Michel
75006 Paris   Tel. 43.25.91.19
Librairie du Commerce International
10, avenue d'Iéna
75016 Paris   Tel. 40.73.34.60
Librairie Dunod
Université Paris-Dauphine
Place du Maréchal de Lattre de Tassigny
75016 Paris   Tel. (1) 44.05.40.13
Librairie Lavoisier
11, rue Lavoisier
75008 Paris   Tel. 42.65.39.95
Librairie L.G.D.J. - Montchrestien
20, rue Soufflot
75005 Paris   Tel. 46.33.89.85
Librairie des Sciences Politiques
30, rue Saint-Guillaume
75007 Paris   Tel. 45.48.36.02
P.U.F.
49, boulevard Saint-Michel
75005 Paris   Tel. 43.25.83.40
Librairie de l'Université
12a, rue Nazareth
13100 Aix-en-Provence   Tel. (16) 42.26.18.08
Documentation Française
165, rue Garibaldi
69003 Lyon   Tel. (16) 78.63.32.23
Librairie Decitre
29, place Bellecour
69002 Lyon   Tel. (16) 72.40.54.54

GERMANY – ALLEMAGNE
OECD Publications and Information Centre
August-Bebel-Allee 6
D-53175 Bonn 2   Tel. (0228) 959.120
Telefax: (0228) 959.12.17

GREECE – GRÈCE
Librairie Kauffmann
Mavrokordatou 9
106 78 Athens   Tel. (01) 32.55.321
Telefax: (01) 36.33.967

HONG-KONG
Swindon Book Co. Ltd.
13–15 Lock Road
Kowloon, Hong Kong   Tel. 366.80.31
Telefax: 739.49.75

HUNGARY – HONGRIE
Euro Info Service
POB 1271
1464 Budapest   Tel. (1) 111.62.16
Telefax : (1) 111.60.61

ICELAND – ISLANDE
Mál Mog Menning
Laugavegi 18, Pósthólf 392
121 Reykjavik   Tel. 162.35.23

INDIA – INDE
Oxford Book and Stationery Co.
Scindia House
New Delhi 110001   Tel.(11) 331.5896/5308
Telefax: (11) 332.5993
17 Park Street
Calcutta 700016   Tel. 240832

INDONESIA – INDONÉSIE
Pdii-Lipi
P.O. Box 269/JKSMG/88
Jakarta 12790   Tel. 583467
Telex: 62 875

IRELAND – IRLANDE
TDC Publishers – Library Suppliers
12 North Frederick Street
Dublin 1   Tel. (01) 874.48.35
Telefax: (01) 874.84.16

ISRAEL
Electronic Publications only
Publications électroniques seulement
Sophist Systems Ltd.
71 Allenby Street
Tel-Aviv 65134   Tel. 3-29.00.21
Telefax: 3-29.92.39

ITALY – ITALIE
Libreria Commissionaria Sansoni
Via Duca di Calabria 1/1
50125 Firenze   Tel. (055) 64.54.15
Telefax: (055) 64.12.57
Via Bartolini 29
20155 Milano   Tel. (02) 36.50.83
Editrice e Libreria Herder
Piazza Montecitorio 120
00186 Roma   Tel. 679.46.28
Telefax: 678.47.51
Libreria Hoepli
Via Hoepli 5
20121 Milano   Tel. (02) 86.54.46
Telefax: (02) 805.28.86
Libreria Scientifica
Dott. Lucio de Biasio 'Aeiou'
Via Coronelli, 6
20146 Milano   Tel. (02) 48.95.45.52
Telefax: (02) 48.95.45.48

JAPAN – JAPON
OECD Publications and Information Centre
Landic Akasaka Building
2-3-4 Akasaka, Minato-ku
Tokyo 107   Tel. (81.3) 3586.2016
Telefax: (81.3) 3584.7929

KOREA – CORÉE
Kyobo Book Centre Co. Ltd.
P.O. Box 1658, Kwang Hwa Moon
Seoul   Tel. 730.78.91
Telefax: 735.00.30

MALAYSIA – MALAISIE
Co-operative Bookshop Ltd.
University of Malaya
P.O. Box 1127, Jalan Pantai Baru
59700 Kuala Lumpur
Malaysia   Tel. 756.5000/756.5425
Telefax: 757.3661

MEXICO – MEXIQUE
Revistas y Periodicos Internacionales S.A. de C.V.
Florencia 57 - 1004
Mexico, D.F. 06600   Tel. 207.81.00
Telefax : 208.39.79

NETHERLANDS – PAYS-BAS
SDU Uitgeverij Plantijnstraat
Externe Fondsen
Postbus 20014
2500 EA's-Gravenhage   Tel. (070) 37.89.880
Voor bestellingen: Telefax: (070) 34.75.778

OECD PUBLICATIONS, 2 rue André-Pascal, 75775 PARIS CEDEX 16
PRINTED IN FRANCE
(97 94 01 1) ISBN 92-64-14061-1 - No. 47005 1994